THE ANATOMY OF
LEADERSHIP

IN INDUSTRY 4.0
THE 4.0D® LEADERSHIP DEVELOPMENT MODEL

DR JOHANN UYS
PROF RONNY WEBBER-YOUNGMAN

kr
publishing

INTERNATIONAL
AWARD-WINNING
LEADERSHIP
DEVELOPMENT
MODEL

2021

First published in 2021.

ISBN: 978-1-86922-905-4 (Printed)
eISBN: 978-1-86922-906-1 (PDF ebook)

Published by KR Publishing
P O Box 3954
Randburg
2125
Republic of South Africa

Tel: (011) 706-6009
Fax: (011) 706-1127
E-mail: orders@knowres.co.za
Website: www.kr.co.za

Typesetting, layout and design: Cia Joubert, cia@knowres.co.za
Cover design: Marlene De Lorme, marlene@knowres.co.za
Editing and Proofreading: Valda Strauss, valda@global.co.za
Project management: Cia Joubert, cia@knowres.co.za

For licensing, accreditation and country representation enquiries go to the Contact page on:
www.4-0d.com

"Some are born great, some achieve greatness, and some have greatness thrust upon 'em."

———————

William Shakespeare. Twelfth Night, 1602

TABLE OF CONTENTS

Delve into the need for a new Leadership Development Model that provides a different approach to leadership theorising and modelling. Two commonly held misconceptions about leadership are clarified. The chapter concludes with the WHY behind the 4.0D® Leadership Development Model

Investigate the various approaches to leadership and the influence social dynamics has had on each of the historic leadership theories and models. The chapter ends with an assessment of the relevance and appropriate application possibilities of these for the future, specifically the Fourth Industrial Revolution (4IR) and beyond.

CHAPTER 3: LEADERSHIP, THE 4IR AND BEYOND 42

*Consider the essence of the 4IR, its related technologies, and its implication
on human behaviour, as well as the skills shifts required for leadership
in the future.*

CHAPTER 4: FORMULATING THE 4.0D® LEADERSHIP DEVELOPMENT MODEL: THE THINKING BEHIND THE THINKING 73

*Discover the rationale and reasoning behind the formulation of the 4.0D®
Leadership Development Model and its associated products and processes.*

CHAPTER 5: THE 4.0D® LEADERSHIP DEVELOPMENT MODEL 102

*Explore the comprehensive offering of the 4.0D® Leadership Development
Model and the online 4.0D® Leadership Assessment Protocol.*

FOREWORD

"Leadership, in contrast (to management), is aimed at creating change in what we do and how we do it, which is why leadership is required to work outside established goals, procedures, and structures and explaining to others why it is important to change..." [1]

———————

In today's business environment, much of what we do involves identifying which people to employ, and developing and retaining them. As chief executive officer of Harmony Gold Mining Company Limited ("Harmony" and/or "the Company"), I have a responsibility to create an environment in which our employees are able to strive to be their personal best. I also have a responsibility to invest in our employees to ensure that they are equipped to thrive.

Throughout the company, we have an experienced and competent workforce. We are miners to the core and we understand ore bodies. In today's world however, extracting gold is no longer enough. More is expected of us. We need skills in how to motivate teams, deal with diversity and truly listen. This provides clear context to purpose, while relating to people and persuading them to perform in pursuit of a common goal.

---

[1] *Ibarra, Herminia, Act Like a Leader, Think like a Leader, Boston, Massachusetts; Harvard Business Review Press, 2015, page 36.*

As leaders, our responsibility extends to influencing not only our own workforce, but also the stakeholders with which we collaborate, be they government departments, mining communities, trade unions or shareholders. In the South African gold mining environment, this requires strong leaders who are able to steer Harmony through constant change and challenges.

In line with our company's values of safety, accountability, achievement, of being connected and honest, we fully appreciate that the development of skills is critical to transforming our company and our economy.

Following a rigid screening and vetting process, the Department of Mining Engineering at the University of Pretoria (UP) and Mandate Molefi (under the leadership of Nene Molefi) were selected to assist Harmony in developing leadership skills within our organisation.

Prof Ronny Webber-Youngman, UP's Head of the Department of Mining Engineering and Dr Johann Uys, senior lecturer in UP's Department of Mining Engineering and Senior Researcher in Leadership in the 4th Industrial Revolution, have been tasked with equipping our workforce with practical leadership guidelines – a toolkit on leadership to supplement our mining toolkit! Besides being academics, they are also leadership practitioners who recognise our need for a less theoretical approach, and train using more hands-on guidelines on how to lead in various situations and in different capacities.

The Harmony leadership development program started in October 2017 and involves our junior, middle and executive management cadre.

Harmony was the first company to be exposed to the 4.0D® Leadership Development Model that formed part of our leadership development program. The program consists of five study schools, which cover the following themes: Harmony ambassador, leading self, leading others, the versatile leader and delivering results.

The 4.0D® Leadership Development Model focuses on self-awareness and acquiring the skills necessary to adapt leadership practices to different circumstances. The model is assisting Harmony in creating leaders who are more balanced, and who have a better understanding of themselves and how their actions affect and influence others, at work or elsewhere.

While the programme is still ongoing, during the period 2017 to 2020, a total of 267 junior managers, 106 senior managers and 35 general managers and/or executives of Harmony have benefitted from this process.

There is no doubt that the book you are holding will transform you. This compact book comprises a review of leadership theories and models spanning several centuries. The authors highlight the usefulness of these theories in the contemporary world of industry. The book covers Industry 4.0 and beyond, with specific emphasis on the skills needed to adapt in an ever-changing environment. This book provides you with leadership 'laws' that are proven to be timeless, sustainable pillars to lead in the modern world. An organisation is managed for the benefit of a myriad of stakeholders, including shareholders; this publication will assist you in attaining a return on investment, through the development of your employees' leadership skills.

The authors are established and proficient leaders, who have trained numerous managers and senior executives in leadership, and have witnessed the subsequent transformation of companies. Their approach is grounded in science and the visual tetrahedron design, which is at the centre of the model, makes leadership development easy to understand.

UP has assisted Harmony in developing courageous, ethical leaders across all levels who are equipped to speak up, speak out and make integrated decisions that will result in a meaningful difference in the industry and the countries in which we operate.

As Harmony, we are honoured to be part of the leadership development journey in South Africa. Read this book, apply it and witness the transition in your company. Harmony's success is testimony to the fact that it is well worth investing in leadership development.

Peter Steenkamp
Chief Executive Officer
Harmony Gold Mining Company Limited

PREFACE

This model, together with its associated products and processes, is the result of the authors' personal leadership experience as well as their mentoring of leadership trainers and developers. The experience of the authors spans more than two decades. To this end, the "science" of the 4.0D® Leadership Development Model is epistemologically intact and peer reviewed. It has also been published in the following accredited journals:

> Uys, J. & Webber-Youngman, R. (2019). A 4.0D Leadership Development Model postulation for the Fourth Industrial Revolution relating to the South African mining industry. *Journal of the South African Institute of Mining and Metallurgy*.
>
> ———
>
> Uys, J. & Webber-Youngman, R. (2020). A 4.0D Leadership Development Model for mining and related industries in the context of the Fourth Industrial Revolution. *Mining Report. Gluckhaüf* 1: 156. pp 21–29.

The 2020 peer reviewed paper, published in Germany, is subsequent to a presentation on the 4.0D® Leadership Development Model by the authors at the 30th International Conference and Annual General Meeting of the Society of Mining Professors (SOMP) in July 2019.

This society represents most universities that have mining engineering training schools. The Society bestowed the Bruce Hebbelwhite Award on the paper. Part of the citations reads as follows:

"The award recognises author(s) presenting papers at the SOMP Annual General Meeting (AGM), for their contributions to the body of knowledge".

PREAMBLE

As a Dubai-based global company, Talent Expertise International (TEI) provides professional services to its clients in Europe, Africa, the Middle East and the Far East. The consultancy delivers services to its clients in 26 cities around the globe. One of its focus areas is leadership development on all levels.

The fast-moving pace of change in industry these days has a vast impact on the domain of leadership development. However, this provides TEI with a fantastic opportunity to collaborate with the world's best leadership development practitioners and consultants, as well as with leading universities and thought leaders. Through these partnerships, we constantly seek the best of the best to integrate into our programmes for the benefit of our clients. These innovative programmes will excite, add value and transform individuals, groups and organisations to meet challenges of the exciting times that lie ahead.

When we came upon the 4.0D® Leadership Development Model, the 4.0D® Leadership Assessment Protocol and the in-training tool, the 4.0D® Leadership Visual Device, we immediately embraced this new approach as the flagship product in our leadership development offering to all our clients. This approach will become the trigger point of departure for all leadership journeys not only at TEI. We predict that it will grow into a standard for all leadership development practices throughout the world.

John Philp
Chief Executive Officer
Training Expertise International

XII

CHAPTER 1:
INTRODUCTION

"Character cannot be developed in ease and quiet. Only through experiences of trial and suffering can the soul be strengthened, vision cleared, ambition inspired, and success achieved."

Helen Keller

THE 4.0D® LEADERSHIP DEVELOPMENT MODEL

This book will introduce you to the novel 4.0D® Leadership Development Model. In a world in constant flux, and where people come with their own blend of attributes, we foresee this model becoming one of the main contributors in the field of leadership and leadership development. To be relevant in the next few decades, anyone involved in leadership development will have to embrace drastic transformations in their approach to every area of leadership development modelling, training and development. It is for exactly that purpose that we developed this model. With the 4.0D® Leadership Assessment Protocol, as well as the 4.0D® Leadership Development Model Visual Device, a new leadership developmental journey has come to fruition. This book will take you on the first steps towards cultivating your own personal blend of leadership skills towards the future of 4IR and beyond.

Among mountains of leadership theories, models and postulations, you will find stacks of oversimplified, clichéd recipes or approaches packaged as "seven easy steps to leadership" or "five essentials of leadership" among a plethora of similar titles. This book excludes those.

Collectively, most programmes claim that leadership competencies and skills can be acquired very easily through one of the many popular programmes that are available as self-study or online courses. Most of these guarantee a return on investment for the effort and cost of participation, while others promise an instant answer to what it takes to become a leader – or even a better leader. Other academically intact leadership development journeys provide a vast array of skills, competencies, evaluations, assessments, education, courses, forums, literature, seminars and workshops, coaching and mentoring on how to be a great leader.

The content of these offerings usually range from traditional managerial programmes that cover planning, organising, leading and control, further supplemented by a range of content on marketing, economics and finances, administration, strategy, business law, supply chain and logistics management programmes that assert to deliver well-rounded leaders. However, the closest these come to the leadership of people could perhaps be if human resources and business communication were also included. The question remains, however, if these types of offerings do indeed yield good leaders, why are leadership failures in virtually all industries and sectors of the world economy (and even politics globally) so rife? One reason could be that leadership development has remained stagnant since the turn of the century. As a result, leadership training and development are the same today as they were 20 or even 40 years ago! These skills, competencies and trained attributes aim to provide executive learners with knowledge of all the necessary leadership paradigms. Yet, are they truly effective and sustainable?

Still, people consume these programmes with relish, but virtually no recent programmes provide any significant or fresh insights into new skills and management methodologies, and little evidence manifests of new leadership behaviours in the workplace. However, few (if any) of these programmes distinguish between *knowing* and *doing*, as well as perhaps the hardest leadership "skill" to master: individual personal readiness for leadership, leadership roles and leadership responsibilities. None of these leadership development programmes truly focus on personal psychological development. Note the emphasis on development and not analysis. Psychometrics is part of this analysis fad, and no programme transcends beyond analysis to achieve psychological balance, wellness and awareness through authentic insight into the self.

This book also excludes all of the above and this model offers none of the quick fixes promised by these programmes. It rather represents what an executive on one of our leadership programmes aptly labelled as a model that "...comes as a diamond in the scratch patch of attractive but worthless gemstones".

What the world needs now is a new leadership development model to provide an answer to the foreseeable future leadership challenges to embrace the 21st century with confidence and success. Contemporary leadership environments are too fraught with change and uncertainty. Thus, yesteryear's success will count for little in tomorrow's world. This means that there is a dire need for a different approach to leadership theorising and modelling.

For many leaders, this represents foreign territory: a place that will require them to create an entirely new set of reference points. It involves learning a completely new language and new customs. The ability to acquire these unfamiliar navigation points and skills will ultimately determine whether companies will thrive in the contemporary climate or be lost in the jungle forever. The challenging goal is for individuals to realise that all these navigation points actually lie within themselves, not somewhere out there.

This book challenges leaders and leadership developers with one fundamental question: You may be able to change your paradigms and deal with them, but can you shift them? Many may wonder what we mean by this, and here we state: "If you want to go on a leadership journey to learn new things, you need not necessarily change direction or embark on a new route – you must change your thinking and approach to dealing with matters." Hence, leadership development is not complicated. What is required in leadership practice is an inescapable, fundamental and lasting shift in behaviour, thinking and emotions. This is the shift that is so necessary for the future because without it, the 4th Industrial Revolution will bring potentially disruptive leadership scenarios.

The intention of this book is not to offer previous learning, which many may have been exposed to in MBA or management development programmes, whether on junior, senior or executive level. What this book offers is insight into a unique model that you can use for your personal development and leadership journey. This will enable you to develop a unique personal leadership identity that will guide you to leadership success.

4

The origins of the 4.0D® Leadership Development Model do not lie purely within the academic world. This journey and its lessons were born in the jungle of leadership in action. Over the years, in our collective and individual contacts with people in leadership development programmes and positions, we have detected a need for new leadership offerings. That is what this book presents.

To start off with, we briefly need to clarify two principles about leadership to enable you to understand the basis of our approach. The first principle is that of three leadership misconceptions that are often encountered when we engage leaders. The second principle is the essence of leadership development programmes as we have experienced it in many organisations with which we have interacted over the last few decades.

LEADERSHIP MISCONCEPTIONS

"Big jobs usually go to the men who prove their ability to outgrow small ones."

Ralph Waldo Emmerson

Traditionally, a leader is the person who is in control of an organisation, a function or other people. In this controlling context, one misconception and stereotype of leadership is that kindness is a weakness. Aspiring leaders often have the notion that to be a dynamic leader and to make a difference means to be a hard driver of people and goals.

That is not true. Leaders can achieve much more by being frank and offering enthusiastic praise for others' *real* performance. By frankly telling people the difficult truth is much kinder than avoiding having difficult and crucial conversations about the facts to protect either them or oneself.

Another misconception is the confusion between personal and positional power. Leadership does not require positional power.

A few simple things build personal power. Two of these are mastering the art of empathetic listening and exercising unconditional positive regard for others. Too often, people judge others based on stereotyping and improper listening.

The last misconception about personal attributes is the distinction between entitlement and ownership. True leaders own their situation – lock, stock and barrel – and do not entitle themselves with the privilege or rank that comes with their status.

THE PRINCIPLE OF A JOURNEY

"Do the best you can until you know better, then, when you know better, do better."

Maya Angelou

The second principle is that leadership development programmes must not be an event individuals attend at some academy and then return to work to practise their new skills sustainably. Leadership development is a lifelong learning journey and a partnership between an individual and their organisation. Leadership development practitioners and delegates need to spend a lot more time applying new knowledge and behaviour to sustain the investment. Organisations must also provide space and time for application to help those leaders sustain and embed their new knowledge and behaviour to form new habits, which, in turn, provide a greater guarantee of sustainability.

New habits successfully form in those organisations that deliberately instil the "learn, apply, reflect" approach to learning. We advocate that this should become part of all organisational learning cultures.
We designed the 4.0D® Leadership Development Model to deal with this through the application of the model during leadership development journeys. Therefore, the structure of the book follows a developmental storyline.

THE "WHY" BEHIND THE 4.0D® LEADERSHIP DEVELOPMENT MODEL

*"There is no greater agony than bearing
an untold story inside you."*

Maya Angelou

Everyone has a story to tell, and around every corner, there is a great story, just awaiting discovery. People must hear them, for – more often than not – stories carry a message, a lesson or wisdom that makes it worthwhile to listen to them. People love to hear stories because nothing is so warm and inviting, yet so challenging and poignant, as a powerful, real-life story.

The story of our Leadership Development Model started in the mid-1990's at one of the big South African mining conglomerates of the time. Those days were characterised by futuristic thinking and fuzzy logic, chaos theory, digital vs analogue, complexity and time span, as well as restructuring. Work at this organisation also entailed getting involved in leadership development at senior and executive level. The corporate mandate enabled collaboration with renowned business schools in South Africa and Europe.

As was standard practice at the time, the incumbents were candidates selected by the corporation to attend a leadership development programme in line with the company's talent pipeline. To become part of that cohort, certain preconditions were in place. They had to have high Assessment Centre results, which would indicate their high potential, and they had to show sufficient cognitive capability and complexity, as determined by an instrument known then as Career Path Appreciation (CPA).

However, not through any fault of the CPA itself, the instrument design or its use and application, but through an unintended consequence, an unforeseen organisational subculture emerged in which CPA results (despite being confidential) caused a division in the ranks between an "in" group and an "out" group.

In addition, these leadership programmes bombarded candidates with an arsenal of psychometrics, covering a vast array of cognitive, interest, motivational and personality profiles.

More than one box file was necessary to carry all the reports. In many instances, there were double assessments in each domain, such as the Myers Briggs Type Inventory (MBTI) and the 16 Personality Factor Questionnaire (16 PF) to determine personality type.

In contact sessions with delegates, it became apparent that the "overkill" of assessments and the confusion it caused among individuals was counterproductive. It seemed that this approach was a way to illustrate that leadership is "difficult". This approach did not offer a clear rationale, it was difficult to find the "why" behind it and this practice just did not feel right.

Over the years of working with leaders in the field of leadership development, our early experiences of leadership development eventually culminated in the model that we propose in this book. Apart from us having raked up a number of reasons to change the status quo, we have also experienced many shortfalls of leadership development outcomes. We are of the opinion that there are future indications that compel the world of leadership development and developers to stand back and seriously review what leadership for the future is really going to be about. This book addresses these in more detail. To this end, Blair Sheppard, in his 2020 book, "Ten years to midnight: Four urgent global crises and their strategic solutions", asserts:

"The world is on the brink of four broad crises that, if not addressed, will cause irreparable harm in the next ten years: a crisis of prosperity, a crisis of technology, a crisis of institutional legitimacy, and a crisis of leadership. All dangerously intertwined, these four crises have forced us to rethink and reconfigure the future.

"Driving that scale of change in today's world will take leadership fit for the task. We need a new model. Leaders need capabilities and sensibilities that seem at odds with each other: technologically sophisticated while also deeply aware of human systems and psychology; heroically courageous, but humble enough to listen and change course if needed; deeply aware of the foundational elements of the things we are trying to change, but highly innovative."

The 4.0D® Leadership Development Model is the departure point for new leadership journeys.

CHAPTER 2:
AN OVERVIEW OF LEADERSHIP THEORY

"The most dangerous leadership myth is that leaders are born – that there is a genetic factor to leadership. That's nonsense; in fact, the opposite is true. Leaders are made rather than born."

Warren Bennis

INTRODUCTION

This chapter provides a synopsis of leadership theory and models. The focus is mainly on those theories that have had a significant impact in leadership development. These theories and models, presented along their developmental and progression timelines, have a specific context and represents the social dynamics of a particular period, which shaped the thinking of the researchers in formulating their assertions.

As far as a definition of leadership is concerned, we concur with Stogdill. As far back as 1974, this Trait theorist asserted that there are as many definitions of leadership as there are researchers and publications on the subject. Since then, this trend has continued, and there are various definitions, each derived from different individual perceptions of leadership based on different research fields. Since researchers define leadership according to their areas of interest and research focus, it would be futile to offer yet another definition of the topic.

However, from the plethora of definitions of leadership, a common strand emerges – that of a person exerting a purposeful influence over individuals and groups in organisations or communities. The objective is usually to guide or coordinate the activities of individuals or groups in a variety of settings in order to reach a goal. A hierarchy exists in the form of leaders having followers or subordinates who are subject to intentional influence. Therefore, there was a time when the calling of a manager and that of a leader separated them.

A supervisor in a factory in the Second Industrial Revolution probably did not have to give much thought to the product or pay attention to the people who were producing it. The job was simply to follow orders, stick to process, organise the work and assign the right people to perform the necessary tasks.

The supervisor then had to coordinate and measure results, and ensure that employees did their job. The focus was on efficiency and production targets, not people. At the time, people were not regarded as an important factor and the focus was rather on optimised output by humans operating machines or using tools and equipment to produce objects.

In the new economies of the Third Industrial Revolution, companies realised that value would come increasingly from the knowledge of people. Workers were not gears in an industrial machine and, consequently, the separation of management and leadership did not come easily. It therefore makes more sense to differentiate broadly between leadership and management rather than to define either one of them individually. The two concepts are often confused or used interchangeably; and people often wonder whether the one represents the other.

While there are hundreds of opinions on the differences between management and leadership, industry leaders following our leadership development programmes over the past two years have listed 15 common perceptions as follows:

MANAGEMENT	LEADERSHIP
Planning	Visioning
Organising	Facilitating
Leading (teams)	Actuate other's aspirations
Control	Setting direction
Budgeting	Future focus
Technical know-how	Develop others
Focus on goals	Focus on vision and meaning
Focus on tasks	Focus on relationships
Production focus	Process focus
I am the boss	Mediate, facilitate, coach, mentor
Positional power	Personal power
Telling	Listening
Compliance	Pioneer
Subordinates	Followers
Operations	Strategies

Table 1: The difference between managers and leaders

Without stating the obvious, what is evident from the sets of perceptions presented above, is that managers and leaders often require elements of both qualities from time to time. One of the reasons for this is that, as organisations go through their respective cycles and phases of business challenges, the relevance and appropriateness of each will come into play at different times. Whereas managers were required to make organisations successful in the 20th century, the 21st-century leader will have to become much more innovative and move away from the previous century's organisational practises and take action in the contexts that the Fourth Industrial Revolution (4IR) and beyond will bring. It has also become quite clear that, in the context of the comparison of the two sets of qualities, one can no longer use one or the other in isolation. Cross-functional qualities will become more and more important as the challenges with regard to leadership become more intense.

One of the questions that arises, however, is "If there are, in fact, aspects about leadership that must be abandoned, changed or transformed to shape a new approach to leadership; what are they? To achieve more clarity on this question, the origins of the various theories and models, and an overview of leadership, warrant attention, since much of current leadership thinking is rooted in its historic origins.

DIVINE RULE

> *"Why do the gods make kings and queens if not to protect the ones who can't protect themselves?"*

George RR Martin

Over centuries, through archival analyses of scripts and scrolls, it would appear that leadership is a phenomenon applicable to humanity as a whole. Almost all tribes, peoples, societies or nations throughout the ages have had various forms of leaders, predominantly enforced via unassailable royal status. Royals ruled because they – and their noble households and families – claimed that their occupation of this station came about by having been "chosen" or "anointed" by some or other divine body to rule over others. At the same time, this anointment by a God or Supreme Being secured the royal station since nobody could challenge or question the divine appointment. This protection made the leadership role or status of monarchs, kings, sultans and emperors irrefutable.

To maintain their superior and absolute leadership positions and standing, rulers – with a variety of titles, such as kings and queens, tsars, sultans, emperors, sovereigns, monarchs and imperators – invariably appointed their political and military leaders from within their own clan since their family circles were the most trustworthy. Strong bonds with the ecclesiastical class prevailed because the link to their divine ruler ensured the status quo of divine rule over others. This practice prevailed for centuries, and to preserve this, the custom warranted many wars and conflicts among nations and peoples of the world. The result of kings (and queens) declaring war on each other flowed into the armies of the kings. Apart from the fact that their own kin and families were generals and commanders of their armies, they were also office bearers in political roles.

From this, records show the first evidence of leadership theory – the so-called "Great Man" theories.

"GREAT MAN" THEORIES (1840'S)

"I grow daily to honour facts more and more, and theory less and less. A fact, it seems to me, is a great thing; a sentence printed, if not by God, then at least by the devil."

Thomas Carlyle

Leadership annals by the Scottish philosopher and historian Thomas Carlyle in the 1840's describe the profiles of highly influential and unique individuals whose actions and deeds had decisive historical effects. At that time, psychology was in its infancy and psychometrics was virtually non-existent. Leadership, as a field of study, emerged from observations and descriptions of important office bearers' actions and their leadership behaviour of influence, impact and effect. The divine right still prevailed, and at that time, many leadership labels emerged: military, religious, political – all connected to some royal status. The basis for the "Great Man" Theories is the assumption that great leaders are born and not nurtured or developed. Leadership is therefore intrinsic to an individual's genetic make-up and royal connections. The phrase "Great Man" was coined in terms of gender, which largely stems from military leaders, where soldiering was an exclusively male occupation.

However, the First World War of 1914–1918 (also known as the Great War) changed this. Prior to this war, only nobility and royals went to military academies. Very few outsiders attended these academies and attendance usually had to carry the blessing of the royal household or its appointed representatives serving on selection boards. Many sources claim that ill-defined goals and inappropriate military strategy and tactics plagued the

Allied campaign during the Great War on virtually all fronts. With this poor planning, insufficient artillery, inexperienced troops, inaccurate maps and poor intelligence led to many defeats on both sides. Officers and generals were mostly overconfident, provisioning inadequate equipment for their troops. Logistical and tactical deficiencies on all levels were commonplace.

One country that played a major role in assisting the Allied forces to win the Great War was the USA. Its military leadership cadres were much more to the point and displayed more strategic expertise and competence. Yet, these commanders were *not* from royalty since America constituted a nation of immigrants rather than royal households that could supply streams of military leaders to command their armies. This brought a new dimension to leadership and effectively ended the postulations of the "Great Man" Theories.

TRAIT THEORIES (1930'S-1940'S)

"To do great things is difficult; but to command great things is more difficult."

Friedrich Nietzsche

Approximately a century later (as psychology developed), leadership theories and research gained momentum. The next generation of theories (albeit similar in many ways to the "Great Man" Theories) is the so-called Trait Theories. These assume that some people inherit certain qualities and traits that make them better suited to leadership than others. It defined intrinsic qualities such as intelligence, sense of duty and responsibility, extroversion, creativity, confidence and even values that – in a composite manner – define the traits of a leader. In the late 1930's to early 1940's, the American personality psychologist, Gordon Allport, identified almost 18 000 English personality-relevant terms.

He postulated the following three trait levels:

- **Cardinal traits:** This is the dominant trait of an individual and shapes a person's behaviour. These can evolve into ruling passions or obsessions, such as a need for money or fame.
- **Central traits:** These traits are general characteristics found to some degree in every person. Central traits are the basic building blocks that shape behaviour. They are not as overwhelming as the cardinal traits. Examples of central traits would be honesty and diligence.
- **Secondary traits:** These characteristics would manifest in certain circumstances (such as particular likes or dislikes that only a very close friend may know). They must be included to provide a complete picture of human complexity.

Since leadership has always been a topic of interest in organisations, societies, communities and nations, the Trait Theories came in very handy at the time. Just as managers in organisations want to explain and understand personality, so they want to understand and explain leaders and leadership. With the advent of the use of psychometrics to measure the personality and behaviour of people, trait leadership flourished.

The Trait Theories underscore the understanding of leadership as a stable series of combinations of personal attributes. Based on personality typologies, these cognitive and behavioural responses to circumstances and environments prevailed for decades. Many branches of Trait Theories evolved. In the context of the Trait Theories, two psychologists, David

McClelland and Douglas McGregor, added significantly to the realm of leadership in 1961.

David McClelland posed his Achievement Motivation Theory of the 1940's in a revised form as part of the Trait Theories. Although originally intended to elaborate on and explain human motivation, he asserted three needs that manifest in leadership: achievement, power and affiliation.

- **Need for Achievement (nAch)**

This need stems from the unconscious concern to achieve through individual effort and excellence. High nAch individuals have an internal locus of control and display traits such as self-confidence and high energy. In their pursuit of realistic and achievable goals, they will take responsibility to solve problems and take calculated risks. They are hardworking and diligent.

- **The need for Power (nPow):**

People with nPow will seek positions of authority because of an unconscious need to influence others through control and dominance. While they have high energy levels and self-confidence, they channel it into competitiveness and, as a result, resent losing. In the process of satisfying their need for power, they will confront opposition and constantly seek win-lose situations.

- **Need for Affiliation (nAff)**

This unconscious need relates to seeking, establishing, restoring and maintaining close personal relationships. These individuals tend to be sensitive to others. By joining organisations and groups, they actively seek opportunities to help others because of a desire to be liked and accepted by others.

In 1966, McGregor postulated Theory X and Theory Y. He based it on a leader's attitude towards their followers. Theory X asserts that people are inherently lazy and lax, and need constant supervision to complete tasks. Theory Y, on the other hand, accepts people as hard working because they like working hard and therefore need no or very little supervision.

It is questionable whether McGregor's leadership theory is actually in the domain of the Trait Theories or whether it is just another contribution on motivation in the work context with reference to manager-subordinate roles. The manager versus subordinate is very typical of the behavioural and situational theories that will follow later in this chapter, and is not so much part of the Trait Theories school of thinking.

The main criticism against the Trait Theories is simply that there are vast numbers of people who possess traits associated with leadership, yet not everyone who possesses these qualities seeks out positions or aspires to any form or level of leadership. The central question raised by antagonists of the Trait Theory is simply: "If particular traits are key features of leadership, how do we explain people who possess those qualities but are not leaders?"

In addition, Trait Theory did not really achieve the desired list of useful leadership qualities as a basis for isolating leadership qualities and characteristics in all contexts, nor have these traits proved themselves static and constant over time. One question that the Trait Theories is not very clear on is: "Do these traits make leaders, or do leadership positions cause individuals to develop these traits?"

Furthermore, Trait Theory is sensitive to contamination by other theories. An example is McClelland's motivational theories, which invaded the leadership space while it initially intended to explain the reasons why people do certain things in an interpersonal context. These stem from needs that are unconscious drivers of behaviour to gain the upper hand. At most, the need for power is a management rather than a leadership trait. Furthermore, the need to affiliate is not a leadership-appropriate methodology. A leader would rather create an organisational context and culture that would accommodate the affiliation and assimilation of individuals automatically or naturally.

The main value of Trait Theory is dispositional traits, the core of which is habitual patterns of behaviour, thought and emotion. Chapter 5 will elaborate on this in more detail.

BEHAVIOURAL THEORIES (1940'S TO EARLY 1960'S)

"Leaders aren't born, they are made. And they are made just like anything else, through hard work. And that's the price we'll have to pay to achieve that goal, or any goal."

Vince Lombardi

In its early years, psychology and its behavioural principles were largely based on the case analyses of pathology, and several formulations arose from this, most notably, Sigmund Freud's patient interaction descriptions, such as the case of Anna O.

In times to follow, psychology developed as a science through research on behaviour, and behaviourists asserted that the study of behaviour should be a natural science such as chemistry or physics.

BF Skinner, who studied operant conditioning (reward and punishment) as a way to shape people's conditioned responses or behaviours in the 1940's, is widely regarded as the father of behavioural theories. Parallel to gaining more knowledge on behaviour and personality, a need to measure for the prediction or assumptions of human behaviour evolved. This gave rise to more sophisticated psychometrics, especially with the statistical methods of factor analysis that would enable the more accurate pinpointing of, among other factors, critical leadership variables in people.

As such, behavioural leadership theory focuses on the actions of successful leaders, not on mental qualities or internal states. Thus, in the context of the rise of behaviourism, it asserts that people can be trained ("conditioned" in behavioural terms) to become leaders. This approach diametrically opposes the theories of the previous century, which stuck to the "leaders are born" adage. Apart from teaching leadership, it also develops by observing the behaviour of role models.

Management theorists Robert Blake and Jane Mouton developed the managerial or leadership grid in the early 1960's. This grid shows a bi-axial grid that plots the degree of task-centeredness versus person-centeredness. In doing so, it identifies five different combinations of the two and the styles they produce.

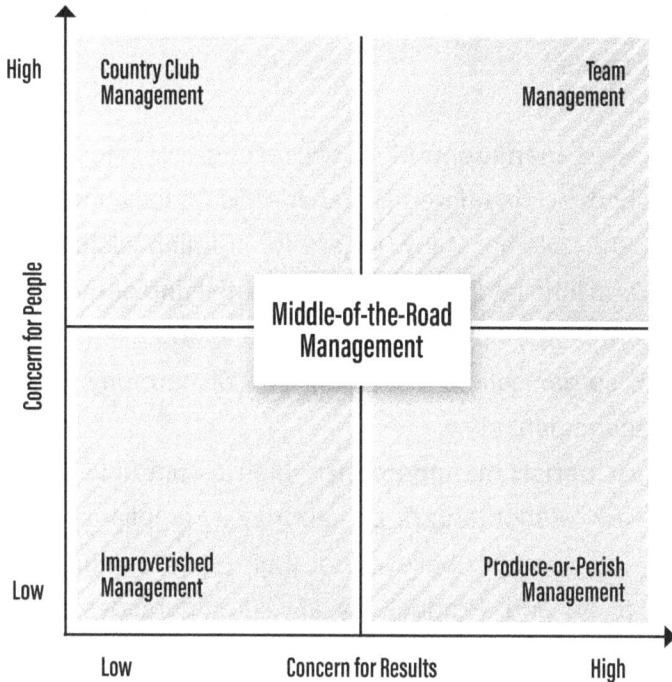

Figure 1: Blake and Mouton's managerial grid

Blake and Mouton's managerial grid elaborates on two behavioural dimensions:

- **Concern for people – Y-axis:** This is the degree to which a manager considers team members' needs, interests and areas of personal development when deciding how best to accomplish a task.
- **Concern for results – X-axis:** This is the degree to which a manager emphasises concrete objectives, organisational efficiency and high productivity when deciding how best to accomplish a task.

From these two axes, Blake and Mouton identified the following five management styles:

1. **Impoverished management** – low results/low people focus: The impoverished or "indifferent" manager is mostly ineffective. This management style has a low regard for creating systems to get the job done, and little interest in creating a satisfying or motivating team environment or attempting to balance the team's needs with the goal outputs. Disorganisation, discontent and disharmony are outcomes of this management style.

2. **Produce-or-perish management** – high results/low people focus: Labelled as "authoritarian" or "authority-compliance" managers, people in this category believe that their team members are simply a means to an end. Productivity always supersedes the needs of the team or its members. Being autocratic, this type of manager has strict work rules, policies and procedures. They believe that punishment is an effective way to motivate team members. While this approach drives impressive production results at first, low team morale and motivation will ultimately emerge. This will affect people's performance and this leader will struggle to retain high performers.

3. **Middle-of-the-road management** – medium results/medium people focus: A middle-of-the-road or "status quo" manager tries to balance results and people. However, this strategy is not as effective as it may sound. Through continual compromise, this leader will fail to inspire high performance, as well as meeting people's needs fully. The result is that the team will likely be characterised by mediocre performance.

4. **Country club management** – high people/low results focus: The country club manager is "accommodating" and their main concern revolves around the team members' needs and feelings. This manager assumes that, as long as subordinates are happy and secure, they

will give their best. The result tends to be a work environment that is very relaxed with much fun, but where productivity suffers due to a lack of direction and control.

5. **Team management** – high production/high people focus: Team management is the most effective style according to the grid. It reflects a person who has managed to find the perfect balance between being equally passionate about work and people, and who does the best they can for the team. These team (or "sound") managers can commit to their organisation's goals and mission. They are able to motivate people reporting to them and work hard to get people to stretch themselves to deliver exceptional results. In addition, they are inspiring figures who care for their teams. Team members feel respected and empowered and are committed to achieving their goals. Team managers create a balance between the organisation's production needs and their people's needs by clarifying the organisation's purpose for their team members and involving them in determining production needs.

The model assumes that the needs of people who are committed to and who have a stake in the organisation's success coincide with the production needs. It further assumes that the result would be an environment based on trust and respect, and consequently high employee satisfaction levels, motivation and achieving – and even exceeding – goals.

After Mouton's death in 1987, Blake and his colleagues added the following two additional dimensions to the grid, although neither appear on the grid itself:

- **Paternalistic management:** A paternalistic manager lies between the country club and produce-or-perish leadership styles. This type of leader can be supportive and encouraging, but will also guard their own position – and paternalistic managers do not appreciate anyone questioning the way they think. While it does not replace the middle-of-the-road manager, the position could be anywhere on the continuum.

- **Opportunistic management:** This management style is not on the grid because it can show up anywhere within the grid. Opportunistic managers place their own needs first. They shift around the grid to adopt whichever style will benefit them at any given time. They tend to manipulate and take advantage of others to get what they want.

While the model itself is a fairly simplistic and plain offering, its consideration of only two variables – work and people – is limited. Furthermore, the alternative styles people can adopt are not sustainable in all instances. This means that when managers and leaders deliberately adopt a style, the chances are very high that when things go wrong, the acquired or learnt style will disappear when the individual defaults to his or her natural or instinctive leadership styles.

Furthermore, the addition of the paternalistic and opportunistic management styles illustrates the initial design flaw of the model. Other factors such as organisational culture and human decision making are not in the grid offering. Perhaps styles should differ from time to time depending on the nature of the work. In certain situations, a more task-oriented approach might not be as insufficient as one would assume.

CONTINGENCY THEORY OF LEADERSHIP (1960'S-1970'S)

"It seems to me that everything that happens to us is a disconcerting mix of choice and contingency."

Penelope Lively

Fiedler pioneered a theory that proposes that a leader's effectiveness hinges on how well their leadership style matches the current context and task. Fiedler agrees with two different styles of behavioural theories: the task-oriented and the people-oriented theories. The effectiveness of a person's style in a particular situation depends on how well defined the job is, how much authority the leader has, and the relationship between the followers and the leader. The contingency theory of a leader and people in making decisions is often referred to as the normative decision theory, as postulated by Vroom and Yetton.

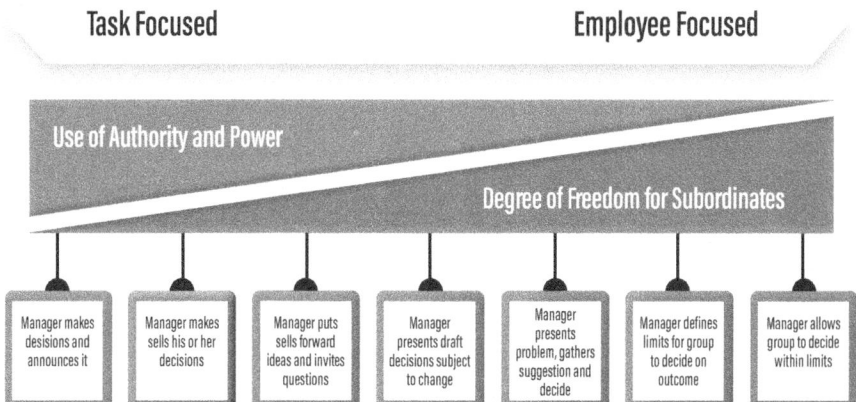

Task Focused				Employee Focused		
Use of Authority and Power				Degree of Freedom for Subordinates		
Manager makes desisions and announces it	Manager makes sells his or her decisions	Manager puts sells forward ideas and invites questions	Manager presents draft decisions subject to change	Manager presents problem, gathers suggestion and decide	Manager defines limits for group to decide on outcome	Manager allows group to decide within limits

Figure 2: The contingency or normative decision theory

Fiedler's contingency theory, like all contingency theories, states that there is no singular best way to lead a team, but that the situation will determine the best way. In Fiedler's contingency theory, it is important to realise that leadership styles are fixed. Styles cannot change to suit the situation; instead, it is better to place leaders in situations that match their styles, but this is not so easy due to a variety of settings that usually prevail in complex organisations.

Paradoxically, other contingency theories determine that leadership and the leadership styles adopted are the most appropriate or most likely to achieve the most successful outcome, given the specific variables in a particular environment. This puts Fiedler's approach at odds with other contingency theory views. In the main, contingency theory is a bit more complex than the previous theories, since it expands beyond the individual's traits and behaviours. It also considers a number of external variables, such as the qualities of the followers, as well as aspects of the work situation.

While the contingency approach to leadership is still popular, it has some criticisms. Firstly, it does not account for the position of the leader within the structure. Secondly, these theories help account for the importance of the situation, but they do not explain the processes behind how leadership styles vary according to the organisation's culture, the many situational variances or features of the group.

SITUATIONAL THEORIES (1970'S-1980'S)

"It is not enough to describe your leadership style or indicate your intentions. A situational leader assesses the performance of others and takes the responsibility for making things happen."

Paul Hersey

The situational theory, developed by Paul Hersey and Ken Blanchard, first introduced in 1969 as the "Life Cycle Theory of Leadership", was renamed the "Situational Leadership Theory" in the mid-1970's.

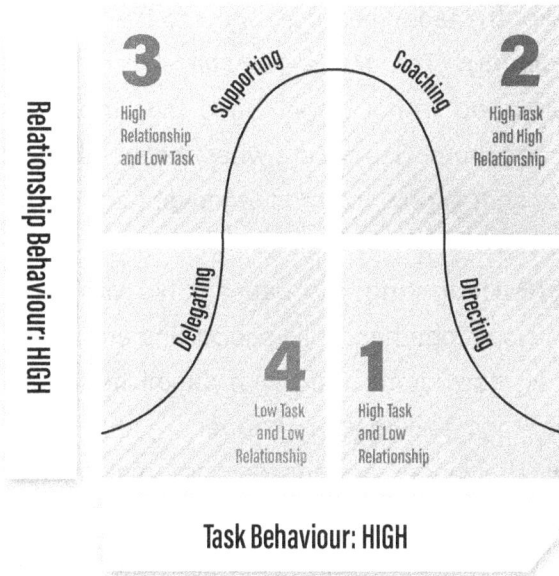

Figure 3: Hersey and Blanchard's Situational Leadership Theory

Very similar to the Contingency Theories, Situational Theories merely expand to the specific appropriateness of the various styles of a specific situation, for example, authoritarian (in a crisis) vs. participative (in a team context). These theories assume behaviour control: Leaders can change their behaviour at will to meet different circumstances. In addition, it repeats the two factors of work (directive behaviour) vs people (supportive behaviour) on the same axes as the Behavioural Theories (specifically Blake and Mouton's managerial grid). The difference lies within the specific behaviour needed in a specific situation.

The theory identifies the following four main leadership approaches:

- **Telling/Directing:** This purely entails a directive and authoritative approach. The leader makes decisions and tells employees what to do to enable them to master the task – this may happen when the task is novel or the team member is new to the task.
- **Selling/Coaching:** The leader is still the decision maker, but communicates and works to persuade the employees rather than simply directing them. This occurs when the members start to master the task. The shift is now towards teamwork and team coordination and relationships.
- **Supporting/Participating:** The leader works with the team members to make decisions together, while supporting and encouraging them. This leader is more democratic with diminished focus on the task since, at this stage, task mastery happens.
- **Delegating:** The leader assigns decision-making responsibility to team members, but oversees their work since the team – as individuals – function optimally from a people-and-work balance perspective. This is also known as self-directed work teams.

In addition to these four approaches to leadership, Hersey and Blanchard also describe the following four stages of follower maturity:

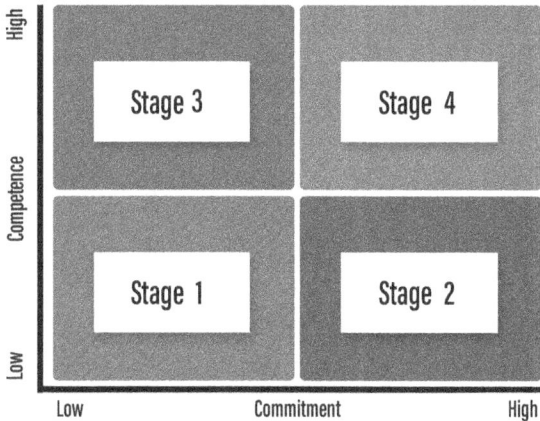

Figure 4: Hersey and Blanchard's stages of follower maturity

From Figure 4, it is clear that it is the manager's task to assist and develop subordinates to move through the various stages and reach the ideal state of Stage 4 (high competence-high commitment). In this context, and seen with Hersey and Blanchard's situational model, it is clear that there is no single management or leadership style, but effective leadership is people- and task-relevant and appropriately exercised in the follower maturity context. The most successful leaders are those who adapt their leadership style to the performance-readiness (ability and willingness) of the individuals or teams they lead.

However, in practice, many leaders find this hard to do. Even after lengthy and intensive training, leaders fall back on old behaviours, since unconscious and fixed beliefs, fears or ingrained habits really dictate behaviour. The discretion of what to do in any particular situation is also purely the result of the leader's discretion and situational analyses (which may be wrong or inappropriate).

TRANSFORMATIONAL THEORIES (1980'S)

"The most dangerous people are always clever, compelling and charismatic."

Malcolm McDowell

Transformational theories, also known as relationship theories, are – in essence – the result of the advent of human rights and awareness, and the focus is on the interactions between leaders and followers. This leads to a solid relationship where the main compass is trust. Transformational leaders gain increased levels of motivation from this trust, which enables them to inspire people by helping group members see the importance and meaning of the task. These leaders are focused people who fulfil their potential, but also, through the performance of the group, achieve the required task. Figure 5 shows the various components of transformational leadership.

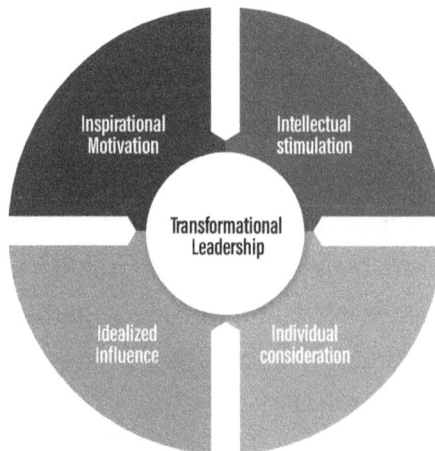

Figure 5: The components of transformational leadership

A challenging essence of transformational theories is the notion of the inspirational nature and charismatic personalities through which leaders transform their followers. Not all leaders can acquire these qualities and therefore elements of Trait Theories remain here.

Leaders are also not always aware of the specific requirements of transformational behaviour and the requirements of the situation at play. In addition, transformational leadership theory does not elaborate on the way to achieve the four different states illustrated in Figure 5.

- **Inspirational motivation:** The foundation of transformational leadership is the promotion of a consistent vision, mission, and a set of values among the members. The vision of transformational leaders is so compelling that they know what they want from every interaction. They guide their followers by providing them with a sense of meaning and challenge. They work enthusiastically and optimistically to foster a spirit of teamwork and commitment.

- **Intellectual stimulation:** Such leaders encourage their followers to be innovative and creative. They encourage new ideas from their followers and never criticise them publicly for the mistakes they make. These leaders focus on the "what" of the problems and do not focus on blaming anyone. They have no hesitation in discarding an old practice set by them if deemed to be ineffective.

- **Idealised influence:** Such a leader believes in the philosophy that he can only influence his followers when he practices what he preaches. Such leaders act as role models that followers seek to emulate. They always win the trust and respect of their followers through their actions. They typically place their followers' needs above their own, sacrifice their personal gains, and demonstrate high standards of ethical conduct. The use of power by such leaders aims at influencing them to strive for the organisation's common goals.

- **Individualised consideration:** Leaders act as mentors to their followers and reward them for creativity and innovation. Followers receive treatment and attention in different ways according to their talents and knowledge. They are empowered to make decisions and get support to implement their decisions.

Transformational leaders have a charismatic appeal, but charisma alone is perhaps insufficient for changing and then sustaining the way an organisation operates. Furthermore, because rules and regulations are flexible, rather than guided by group norms, the likelihood of coercion and manipulation is a risk. While these attributes may very well provide a sense of belonging for the followers as they can easily identify with the leader and its purpose, they can also lead to corruption and deviant group norms.

The case study that follows illustrates the transformational leadership model in an extreme and radically corrupted form.

TRANSFORMATIONAL LEADERSHIP: A COERCION CASE STUDY

David Koresh, (born Vernon Howell in 1959) founded the Branch Davidians – a religious cult with many followers who isolated themselves on a farm in Waco, Texas, USA.

Because of his radical views on theology, the Church of the Seventh Day Adventists expelled him. Koresh claimed to be the Messiah and all women were his spiritual wives. After his rejection by mainstream religion, guitar-wielding David Koresh set up his own cult philosophy, which he named the Branch Davidians, and recruited many like-minded people through his charisma and charm.

Once members, Koresh coerced them to believe that the world would soon end. He indoctrinated his followers in his militant ideas, and they stocked up on an arsenal of firearms to illustrate their militant nature.

His practice of sleeping with church members' wives, prophesising about his self-centred sexual teachings and marrying under-age girls, as well as his large stockpile of weapons and ammunition, drew the attention of both the news media and the federal government.

In March 1993, the Bureau of Alcohol, Tobacco and Firearms (ATF) launched a raid against the cult's compound. A member of the group, out on errand, spotted the agents and police moving towards the compound. He called and warned them, giving them time to arm themselves and barricade their buildings.
When agents and police arrived, they were met with a barrage of small arms fire. They nevertheless attacked the compound. Consequently, ATF agents and six Branch Davidians died in the skirmish and Koresh sustained bullet wounds. The ATF then began a 51-day siege of the compound.

Due to the notoriety of the cult, as well as the attack and loss of life, Cable News Network (CNN) and other news agencies reported daily on the cost of the raid, while public opinion compelled the newly appointed Attorney-General, Janet Reno, to be swift and decisive in her handling of the situation. During the siege, wounded cult members, women and children fled into the waiting arms of government agents.

To force a deadlock, the ATF brought in armoured vehicles and injected tear gas into the compound's main building. A fire broke out and federal agents and local police could only stand by helplessly while the fire consumed the building. The authorities refused to ask the firefighters to expose themselves because of the threat of the ammunition exploding while they attempted to rescue cult members.

In the end, 77 Branch Davidians died in the fire, including Koresh himself and 20 children.

EMOTIONAL INTELLIGENCE (1990'S)

"If your emotional abilities aren't in hand, if you don't have self-awareness, if you are not able to manage your distressing emotions, if you can't have empathy and have effective relationships, then no matter how smart you are, you are not going to get very far."

Daniel Goleman

When Peter Salovey and John D Mayer first published their work on Emotional Intelligence (EI) or Emotional Quotient (EQ) in 1990, they never intended it to be a leadership solution or postulation.

However, in later years, they started expanding it to leadership after Daniel Goleman's 1995 book, *"Emotional intelligence: Why it can matter more than IQ".*

Salovey and Mayer rather contributed the identification of a set of skills that enables people to accurately appraise and express emotions in themselves, as well as in others, and to use feelings to motivate and plan for achieving things in life and to master better coping strategies.

When Daniel Goleman published his book in 1995, he elaborated extensively on EQ and explained it to such an extent that people regard him as the father of EQ and not Salovey and Mayer.

Salovey and Mayer's initial premise was that EI gives one the following:

- The ability to perceive and correctly express one's emotions and those of other people
- The ability to use emotions in a way that facilitates thought
- The capacity to understand emotions, emotional language and emotional signals
- The ability to manage one's emotions in order to achieve goals

Reuven Bar-On, an Israeli psychologist, then developed a way to measure EQ. His emotional social intelligence (ESI) assessment instrument measures various dimensions of EQ.

EQ-I SCALES	THE EI COMPETENCIES AND SKILLS ASSESSED BY EACH SCALE
Intrapersonal	Self-awareness and self-expression
Self-regard	To accurately perceive, understand and accept oneself.
Emotional self-awareness	To be aware of and understand one's emotions.
Assertiveness	To effectively and constructively express one's emotions and oneself.
Independence	To be self-reliant and free of emotional dependency on others.
Self-actualisation	To strive to achieve personal goals and actualise one's potential.
Interpersonal	Social awareness and interpersonal relationship
Empathy	To be aware of and understand how others feel.
Social responsibility	To identify with one's social group and cooperate with others.
Interpersonal relationship	To establish mutually satisfying relationships and relate well with others.
Stress management	Emotional management and regulation
Stress tolerance	To effectively and constructively manage emotions.
Impulse control	To effectively and constructively control emotions.
Adaptability	Change management
Reality testing	To objectively validate one's feelings and thinking with external reality.

Flexibility	To adapt and adjust one's feelings and thinking to new situations.
Problem solving	To effectively solve problems of a personal and interpersonal nature.
General mood	**Self-motivation**
Optimism	To be positive and look at the brighter side of life.
Happiness	To feel content with oneself, others and life in general.

Table 2: Bar-On's dimensions of emotional social intelligence

In short, emotional intelligence is an array of non-cognitive proficiencies, competencies and skills that unlock the individual's abilities to use this information to guide their thinking and action.

Since emotional intelligence was a relatively new contribution to the world of leadership, it focused on social context behaviour and was not aimed exclusively at leadership. The emphasis was rather to place personal effectiveness and success on a continuum as underscored by Bar-On's ESI assessment instrument.

By using that information, individuals can develop their weaknesses and harness their EQ strengths. Although not formulated to be a leadership theory or model, it has very strong elements to apply in the field of leadership. Many people assert that the extremely high importance of EQ for leadership is debatable as it is not the only factor or the centre of the leadership universe.

CONCLUDING REMARKS

"That challenge you have right now...it's not a wall; it's a door. It's meant to be opened. Get a handle on the situation and open it."

Richie Norton

The theories reviewed in this chapter have contributed significantly to the understanding and development of leadership, and have served leadership development programmes for a long time. However, they have reached the end of their shelf life, having led to conventional thinking about leadership in the mindset of a conventional world. Conventional leadership mindsets in traditional hierarchical organisational contexts have created organisational cultures that are slow to change and slow to respond to doing things differently. Hierarchies have also created comfort zones with the subsequent inability of leadership in industries to make paradigm shifts. Together, these factors are hampering the requisite leadership that organisations or industries need for the future. This is very evident in industries that are littered with examples of leadership failures. The reasons for these failures are largely due to a history of "management knows best".

Furthermore, not one leadership theory or model examines the individual as a holistic person. At most, EQ touches upon certain aspects of it by connecting cognition and emotion. Trait Theory acknowledges habitual patterns of behaviour, thought and emotion. Yet, it does not include the dynamics and interactive nature of the emotional, thought and behavioural triad.

No model or theory describes certain human "laws" or "rules" as the foundation of where leadership all begins. In short, in none of these theories is there a link between an individual's personal dynamics and leadership. In this vein, organisations continue to prepare individuals for leadership in the 21st century with models and theories that pre-date the now obsolete fax machine. If this persists, leadership may fail on an increasing scale.

The 21st century requires a new kind of leader. There is an increasing realisation that the business of most organisations is the business of people. The organisational activities merely represent the playing field of practising this "people business". The nature of work is going to differ radically from current practices in ten to twenty years' time. The basis of leadership theories and models, being tremendously influenced by the prevailing socio-dynamic systems at a particular point in time, makes it evident that current leadership practice, training and development are inappropriate for most organisations. The now Volatile, Uncertain, Complex and Ambiguous (VUCA) world requires new models. The context of increasingly disruptive technologies, Internet of Things, cyber-technology and Big Data add to the current leadership dilemma.

With the advent of the 4IR, it is even clearer that current leadership theory and modelling will be inadequate. A new leadership postulation to cope with these challenges is now imminent. This postulation must be one that explains leadership in new and rapidly changing contexts; one that balances work and people with leadership impact; one that has a solid foundation of balance between individual leadership prowess; and one that clearly spells out leadership direction and objectives as a compass to resilience. Yet, it must be adaptive and agile.

CHAPTER 3:
LEADERSHIP, THE 4IR AND BEYOND

*"Let's go invent tomorrow instead of worrying
about what happened yesterday."*

Steve Jobs

INTRODUCTION

In his opening address at the World Economic Forum (WEF) Congress in 2016, Klaus Schwab, Executive Chairman of the WEF, made the following comment: *"One of the features of the 4IR is that it does not change what we are doing, but it changes us".*

The significance of this statement is quite profound since, never in the history of the world, have changes and the adoption of change been more dramatic than the 4IR is going to demand of people, especially leaders. The way we work, organise and practise various professions and jobs will undergo substantial changes as this revolution expands globally.

Since 1784, the world has progressed through four "industrial revolutions", starting with the First Industrial Revolution (now known as Industry 1.0), progressing through Industry 2.0, Industry 3.0 and – finally – Industry 4.0 (the 4IR).

The 4th Industrial Revolution
(Industry 4.0)

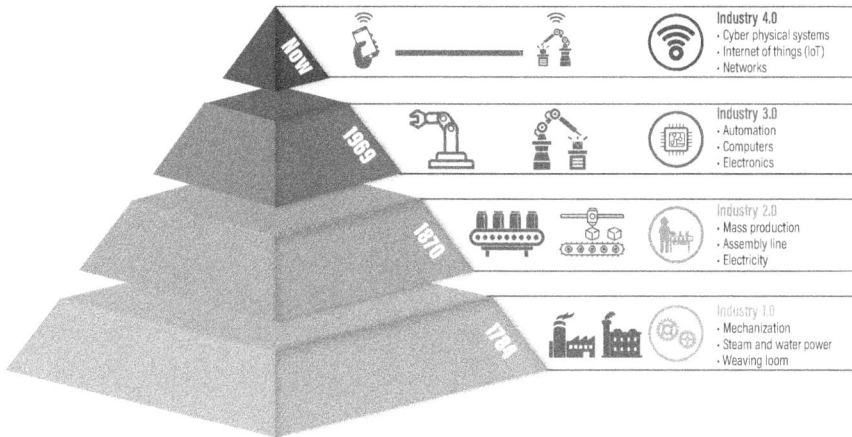

Figure 6: The progression of the various industrial revolutions to date

If one considers the fact that there has been an approximate time span of 200 years between Industry 1.0 and Industry 3.0, and subsequently another 50 years between Industry 3.0 and Industry 4.0, one can anticipate the frequency cycles between revolutions to shorten in future. This makes the adoption of new technologies through a new type of leader, as well as what people do and want in their leaders through new leadership interventions, even more important. The consideration in this chapter of "the 4IR and beyond" is related to the expectation that subsequent industrial revolutions will emerge more frequently in future. In fact, as we will illustrate at the end of this chapter, many futurists believe we are on the brink of entering the Fifth Industrial Revolution (Industry 5.0).

A HISTORICAL OVERVIEW OF THE INTERFACE BETWEEN TECHNOLOGY AND LEADERSHIP

"I know there's a proverb which that says: 'To err is human,' but a human error is nothing to what a computer can do if it tries."

Agatha Christie

The arrival of the personal computer towards the end of the previous century, and later the mobile phone, both proved to be major "disruptors" that heralded the end of Industry 3.0 in a period that is often referred to as the Information Age. Until then, business conduct was in a very traditional and conservative context and the basis for leading people was custom and convention. With the personal computer and ubiquitous Windows Operating System (OS) came the internet. Mobile communication piggybacked on this successful communication system, significantly changing the way the world worked.

Almost overnight, several tried and tested functions and methods became obsolete. The first cracks in the male leadership mantle began to appear. Any individual with access to education and opportunity could now lead; and usually did. In a mirror image of what had transpired with the advent of the printing press, a broader mass of individuals now had access to knowledge and information on an unprecedented scale.

Boardroom information became more freely available to those inside and outside companies in an age where the internet never shuts down. Shareholder activism also began to govern many boardroom decisions.

Two classic examples of information accessibility via technology took place a few years prior to the emergence of the 4IR. The first example was the Chinese government's attempts to restrict news of the outbreak of the deadly Severe Acute Respiratory Syndrome (SARS), but they could not control two billion mobile phone users in China in 2003, and, of course, the story leaked. Another large-scale example was that of Julian Assange, an Australian reporter, editor and publisher, and an information activist, who founded WikiLeaks in 2006. In 2010, he published several sets of information on the US-Iraqi war, and other – some believe clandestine – US-Middle East military activities. The US government, severely embarrassed by these leaks, responded by declaring Assange a fugitive before the law, and launched criminal investigations into WikiLeaks. Thus, connectivity and data were two major catalysts that set the scene for the emergence of the 4IR and beyond.

A HOLISTIC OVERVIEW OF THE ECONOMIC CONTEXTS PRECEDING THE INDUSTRIAL REVOLUTIONS

"Whether it's the best of times or the worst of times, it's the only time we've got."

Art Buchwald

The notion that humans must have leaders has always existed, even before the earliest human commercial activity. Several main economic epochs preceded our entry into man-made industrial revolutions.

EPOCH 1: THE HUNTER-GATHERER ECONOMY

Mankind's first economical activity was not based on commerce, but on survivial. In the world of Homo Sapiens, the fitter, stronger, faster males – who were the best hunters – were the leaders. Formal economic activity was essentially non-existent, but perhaps closest to it was exchanging between groups what they reaped from the earth.

The main activities revolved around women and children foraging for wild vegetation and sourcing what nature could offer, such as honey. Men did the hunting and the fishing. They were nomads who lived from day to day and from meal to meal, and roamed vast tracts of land in search of animals to hunt, mainly by bow and arrow. They needed all their senses of survival, and the ability to move quickly was a survival strategy.

Experience was important. Therefore, the tribe usually regarded the oldest member as the natural leader, the one who had experienced the most springs and seen the greatest number of rainy seasons. Life was harsh; life expectancy was low; and many died in early childhood, especially in the beginning of this epoch before the discovery of medicinal herbs. Man's existence at this stage was geared towards overcoming or mastering skills to cope with nature, while having to survive wild beasts and other hostile tribes.

About 90 000 years of human history belonged to these hunter-gatherers, ending with the rise of the Neolithic Revolution around 12 000 BC, when tribes began to settle and practise agriculture on an increasing scale. Today, we still find hunter-gatherer communities and tribes such as the Hazda People in modern-day Tanzania, the Khoi in South Africa, the Bushmen of the Kalahari Desert, the Spinifex people of the Great Victoria

Desert and the Sentinelese from the Andaman Islands in the Bay of Bengal, to name a few.

EPOCH 2: THE AGRICULTURAL ECONOMY
This epoch emerged when the hunter-gatherer epoch gave way to an economy based on land ownership: the agricultural economy.

The first forms of agriculture emerged about 12 000 years ago. Now, increased mastery over nature, rather than merely physical attributes, was required to become a landowner and the leader on that land. These leaders were predominantly men, and over time, land ownership became a class issue. The right to lead was primarily associated with title, bloodline and privilege – leading to rule by divine right (see Chapter 2). Society became feudal, and autocratic leadership was rife.

Experience in this context also became an important leadership quality. Territories now comprised agricultural production units. Family life and production took place under the same roof and the notion of a cottage industry was born.

Many parts of our world still operate this way: as subsistence economies. Mongolian herders are a good example of such people. This way of life does not focus on the future, but rather on time that simply brings about the changing of the seasons.

EPOCH 3: THE EMERGENCE OF THE INDUSTRIAL ECONOMIES
The emergence of the Industrial Age in the mid-18th century in Britain forever changed both the context and content of work and left an indelible imprint on our understanding of leadership. This era saw the emergence of the factory and the organisation, with its hierarchical structure and

the obvious dichotomy of labour (blue-collar workers) and management/leadership (white-collar workers).

Leaders remained distinctively male and often authoritarian. Fuelled by the Newtonian science of the day, the prevailing worldview was that the world was like a large machine, best understood through analysis, dissection and rational enquiry.

Taylor's book titled *"The principles of scientific management"*, published in 1919, laid the foundation for the decades to follow. This work had a significant influence on the development of the Japanese production techniques of the 1970's, as well as the re-engineering fad that dominated American business in the mid-1990s. The exclusion of women from leadership roles prevailed throughout these years. Leadership still centred on education and privilege. It was autocratic, rigid and controlling – a legacy that in many ways still persists to this day. Many executives remember these years and cling to its principles and residual knowledge.

A NEW EPOCH OF RELATIONAL ECONOMIES OF THE 4IR AND BEYOND

This new epoch demands a very different type of leadership from the old "command and control" style of leadership that ruled virtually every organisation. It requires leaders to be skilled at successfully relating to all kinds of people so that they can set up networks, which have become the new arena in which businesses operate. All indications are that the current competitive differentiating factor will be the quality of our relationships. Relationships take place both inside and outside of business, where people seek *meaning* in why they do things or work. Along with *"how"* these things or work is done, and the related benefits of achieving the *"why"* and the *"how"*, the *"what"* has become more important than ever.

In 2020, the Japanese Council for Science, Technology and Innovation defined Society 5.0 as a human-centered society that balances economic advancement with the resolution of social problems by a system that highly integrates cyberspace and physical space.

Bruno Salgues, in his book "*Society 5.0: Industry of the future, technologies, methods and tools*", published in 2018, amplifies several aspects pertaining to Society 5.0 and the situation of humans in the digital world. Digitisation poses a challenge and an opportunity to a new generation of leaders that needs to embrace and to lead these future societies. A major strength of Society 5.0 is access to information that enhances the ability of skills training. However, one of its key weaknesses is the possibility of information overload. With this comes threats, the main one being the manipulation of information for propaganda purposes. However, the digital world has created many opportunities in both the business and personal world.

Living in a fast, dynamic, technology-driven world requires a very different set of leadership skills. Technology and innovation will require business models to adapt and become agile to make provision for all disruptors, while still operating on a daily basis. Humans need to adapt to the digital world both at work and in their home environment.

We need to understand how living in the digital age will affect us. It is therefore necessary for humans to be aware of the change, look at the opportunities, use these opportunities to educate themselves and be ready for the digital revolution.

To contextualise the requisite leadership skills that will become relevant in the 4IR, the dominant technologies that will drive our lives warrant some attention.

4IR TECHNOLOGIES

"A CD. How quaint. We have these in museums."

Eoin Colfer

One of the main characteristics of the 4IR is that it brings new technologies to the world. These will seemingly cost people their jobs, change the nature of organisations and disrupt the traditional order of things as they have evolved from previous industrial revolutions.

In 2014, Derin Cag founded the website Richtopia. Its goal was to offer in-depth case studies and analyses of leading people and companies to provide both a mass network effect towards, and a wider understanding of future trends. In 2020, Richtopia offers 11 examples of disruptive technologies that are currently at play in the 4IR. Here, we learn that the fast pace of innovation is one of the key challenges of technology in the 4IR.

This indicates that the better leaders adapt to change the quickest, and cements this attribute as one of the key qualities of leaders in the future. The main driver behind the 4IR is digitisation, which will integrate vertical and horizontal value chains, product and service offerings, business models and customer access. This includes disruptive technologies. Leadership and disruption will be two sides of the same coin from now onwards.

Before examining the skills that are required to effectively cope with challenges in the 4IR, it is necessary to consider some of these disruptive technologies.

ADVANCED VIRTUAL REALITY

Virtual reality (VR) is the simulation of a real or imaginative experience or concept that can be different from or similar to the real world. It is applicable to a wide range of fields, such as games, education and training, and even the military. VR is often supplemented (augmented) by related experiences, most of which attempt to enrich the visuals by adding sensory stimulations like olfactory, haptic feedback, and somatosensory and auditory feedback. This refers to Augmented Reality (AR). The next step is Extended Reality (XR), which simply refers to human-computer interfacing.

These technologies relate to the ability to convert data into a format that makes vision visible and makes it possible for everybody else to see what the messenger, manager or leader has in mind. Reality technologies develop at a tremendously rapid pace. What is novel today will most likely be outdated within six months to a year.

VR, AR and XR are largely ubiquitous technologies and, as disruptive technologies, are already making a significant contribution. Perhaps to label it as disruptive has become inappropriate as people have already adopted its uses and applications. Soon VR headsets and related wearables will be ordinary household items for gaming and other visual experiential activities.

ARTIFICIAL INTELLIGENCE

Artificial intelligence (AI) is a select type of intelligence that relates to computers and other machines that "mimic" human beings' natural intelligence. A number of virtual assistant devices are already on the market and operate mainly via smart speakers. They are voice activated with specific key words like "hey Google". The most common virtual assistant examples are Siri, which is part of Apple Incorporated's iPhone, iPad, Apple watches, and Mac and smart television operating systems, and Amazon's Alexa. Alexa does personal chores via a personal computer. She can also become a smart home organiser, switching domestic (and office) devices and appliances on or off upon being requested by the owner from anywhere in the world. Similarly, with Google comes Google Assistant, which is also a personal assistant for users on smart phones, computers and smart devices. Thousands of applications are available for downloading on smart devices and are very common today.

In ordinary households, smart applications can stream from a wide range of platforms that provide videos, documentaries and any conceivable visual or audible content to smart television sets. Smart applications that can connect many devices and even perform domestic chores like dimming lights, switching on heating and drawing curtains and blinds are readily available for domestic use. Connectivity technologies and websites are now common tools and banking and news apps, for instance, have already changed the way people use these services. In the near future, banking branches, as well as printed newspapers and magazines will be obsolete. Debit and credit cards, as a convenient form of payment, are disappearing and are being replaced by secure Quick Response (QR) coding applications for online payments.

An extension of mimicking means machines copy the cognitive functions of the human brain in learning and solving problems. Examples of these are downloadable smart device applications in the form of games (such as chess), driverless cars or autonomous vehicles. However, our view is that machines will never take over human-initiated tasks in the near future because AI is reactive. While it is programmable, algorithms depend on humans for their input since they cannot yet program themselves. The success of AI lies in the capabilities of people to drive the development of the algorithms associated with it. The need for leaders of the future to identify and retain skills related to AI will become an important driver of the success of AI interventions.

INTERNET OF THINGS

The Internet of Things (IoT) is a network of physical objects that uses sensors and Application Programming Interfaces (APIs) to connect and exchange data over the internet. An API is a computing interface, which defines interactions between multiple software intermediaries, and is essentially IoT enabling. Objects equipped with machine-readable identifiers or minuscule identifying devices could dramatically change people's lives.

IoT devices play a significant role in industries such as healthcare, mining, manufacturing and transportation. Derin Cag states that a downside to IoT is that the connections could be vulnerable to present high-security threats, but that IoT as an exciting innovation that warrants more exploration.

However, cyber-space security can mitigate potential security threats. Here, leaders will need to have the ability to "feel" associated with these risks and put strategies in place to deal with the risk accordingly.

The influence of disruptive technology and IoT specifically mentioned here is an important dynamic that leaders will have to deal with in future.

3D PRINTING

Additive manufacturing or 3D printing is one of the most exciting technologies invented and improved upon over the last decade. It has great potential in enhancing production capabilities in many industries. Examples of items already being printed via additive manufacturing technologies are housing settlements, space stations, furniture, utensils, transportation, clothes, games, food, body parts and many more. 3D printing enables organisations to select from a digital inventory storage facility to extract various templates of virtually any object and print it on site. An example is a remote exploration drill rig during the breakdown of a part of the machine. The spare part number contains the technical specification, which can then be printed accordingly on site. This time cycle is much quicker than any conventional supply chain can deliver a replacement part. Thus, 3D printing will disrupt the commercial activity of storing and transporting goods to customers. In addition, 3D printing could disrupt many factories and plants that manufacture 3D-printable products with expensive equipment.

In this, however, lies other opportunities to explore. We think that current 3D printing applications are only the tip of the iceberg. The future uses of 3D printing will change people's lives positively because it is a tool to develop people by making vision visible. There are strong indications that technologies cause people to become increasingly visual learners and interpreters of visual information.

As a developer of others, leaders now gain the ability to build the confidence of their followers in believing, driving and fulfilling the vision they stand for through to a final 3D-printed product. 3D printing is a very symbolic result of a touchable futuristic-thinking vision and ability.

ROBOTICS

Robotics technologies are about machines substituting humans and replicating human actions, as commonly encountered in motor vehicle assembly plants. In robotics, multiple engineering disciplines combine their expertise, for example mechanical with systems engineering. While robotics may replace humans in certain jobs or partly (like a robotic limb in the event of an amputation), robots will not replace people with regard to cognitive functioning, problem solving or emotional aspects related to being human. Robots will not be able to create, program and build robots. People will always design robots and robotics in the context of the specific need of human beings. Robotics in future will play a significant role in creating better environments and related activities in improving peoples' lives, as well as further enhancements in manufacturing in various industry sectors over the world.

According to Cag, robotics relates to robots with enhanced dexterity, sense and intelligence. Robots now perform tasks that are too hard or too dangerous for humans. Although it is currently expensive to automate, societies are already benefitting from this new technology. Robots will always enhance activities related to humans, as well as increase productivity pertaining to manufacturing and other activities.

The concept of robots leading humans belongs to fiction in the context of leadership and the notion of non-robot thinking in leadership. This is evident in the cognitive skills of complex problem solving and creativity. A Leadership Development Model should thus emphasise the need for a sound base (cognition, affect and behaviour) for leaders to understand themselves (as non-robots). These important elements are required in the 4IR and beyond.

BLOCKCHAIN TECHNOLOGY

Satoshi Nakamoto is a pseudonym for the person or group of people that invented blockchain technology in 2011. In 2016, Ameer Rosic described a blockchain as a time-stamped series of immutable records of data that is managed by a cluster of computers not owned by any single entity. Each of these blocks of data (i.e. block) is secured and bound to each other using cryptographic principles (i.e. chain).

Initially designed for financial transactions, where information moves from one point to another and is recorded as blocks, it eventually forms a very transparent set or series of information sets linked to each other as a chain. Each transaction point or block contains information and a unique history about the transaction that cannot be falsified due to the millions of information sets in a chain and sophisticated cryptographic processes. According to Cag, this transformative discovery is a distributed ledger technology that makes blockchain companies like Bitcoin, Stellar (Lumens), Ethereum and others possible by providing a record of transactions and confirming who has what at any given moment. The security of blockchain technology lies in sophisticated cryptographic processes. The impact of blockchain technology may not be apparent to the non-technological eye, but could improve existing systems within society.

However, blockchain transactions are free and have become a threat to other new disruptive technologies of the 4IR. Recent entrants like Uber (the biggest transportation company with no vehicles on its books) and Airbnb (the largest real estate company with no property assets) are under threat. The threat comes from the fact that the only thing to do is to encode the transactional information for a car ride or an overnight stay. This disrupts the matchmaking platform (a service provider connecting directly to a service consumer) by removing the connecting platform and the intermediary's service fee.

From a leadership perspective, the ability to bring together all the related disruptive technologies will become an important skill in the "packaging" of related and beneficial disruptive technologies, putting further emphasis on the ability to "see" the bigger picture. What blockchain will not replace in leadership are the negotiation processes that precede the transactional chains. The decision to partake or not to partake lies, in the end, with the human being.

AUTONOMOUS VEHICLES

The name of this disruptive technology is self-explanatory and comprises automated cars, trucks, buses, boats and drones. Self-driving vehicles use combinations of advanced technologies and sensors such as Light Detection and Ranging (LIDAR), movement sensors, Global Positioning Systems (GPS) and other forms of communication technologies.

In time, autonomous vehicles may serve most industries or public transportation sectors. The benefits pertaining to autonomous vehicles are already evident in many industries.

Autonomous technologies have enhanced information-gathering systems and collect data from the various sensors in the vehicle, which provide information that directs the vehicles to work autonomously. In terms of productivity, as well as economical and safety perspectives, autonomous vehicles have already proven their value and related benefits.

While these vehicles eliminate the possibility of human error in potential vehicle accidents and collisions, they will hardly ever be fully autonomous. People will have to monitor their fleets during movements, control rooms will not disappear and decisions to avoid potential calamities may still have to be human based. These vehicles would perhaps not need humans to upload data, but they will certainly need humans to modify that data as things change over time.

From a leadership perspective, people need instinct; they need to be able to predict situations, and react on impulse as situations unfold. This cannot be pre-programmed. Therefore, technology cannot substitute the ability to make a decision based on gut feel, which developed through experience in the jungle of work. The human response to complex environmental stimuli is very sophisticated and is a quality that develops over time as humans gather experience. Technology cannot gather experience and learn from it. The data technology gathers is for information and data trend analyses. Technology cannot gather data to apply learning and facts in a deductive or inductive reasoning mode.

RENEWABLE ENERGY

The anti-coal-fired power generation sentiments worldwide have opened opportunities in other renewable energy resources, such as solar and wind. Renewable energy resources are still very much (in terms of the costs associated with them) in the "development" phase, with huge expansion potential for the future.

Coal-fired power stations are still the cheapest way to generate electricity, and may remain in use for a very long time. Obviously, the use of renewable energy could reduce the impact of climate change and pollution on a global scale. According to Cag, renewable energy includes inventions such as wind turbines, photovoltaic cells, concentrated solar power, geothermal energy and ocean wave power. Renewable energy is a great example of disruptive technology that will serve the environment and accelerate sustainable development.

The word "renewable" brings to mind notions like "revamp", "improve" or "change for the better". From a leadership perspective, considering the skills and qualities associated with it, the ability to renew and rejuvenate to avoid stagnation is essential. Any form of stagnant mindset would be futile in the context of its use in the 4IR. The 4.0D® Leadership Development Model embraces a dynamic approach, with flexibility and adaptability as a major element for leadership.

MEDICAL TECHNOLOGIES AND PHARMACEUTICAL INNOVATIONS
Medical advances because of digitisation will have an impact on medical disciplines such as virology, immunology and orthopaedics, as well as an array of medical devices. Such devices range from cyber-technological implants and artificial organs to bio-medically manufactured body structures (bones) and organs from the stem cells of individuals.

Surgery and engineering disciplines such as mechanical, electrical/ electronic, mechatronics and systems are increasingly integrated and computer based, with simulations of surgical procedures in preparation for actual theatre work. Hieroglyphics aid organ analyses in a virtual space, and open up immense educational possibilities in the training of surgeons.

Innovations in biochemistry, virology and immunology include vaccines, genomic-directed clinical trials and gene editing, cell-free foetal DNA testing and smart pharmaceuticals. The latter refers to patient care prescriptions of medicine ranges (e.g. hypertension, cholesterol and blood thinning) combined into a single tablet, which is pre-programmed to release the correct medication at the desired time of the day.

The implication of innovations in this field most likely relates to people living longer than ever before, as well as extended career and work-life cycles.

HIGH-SPEED TRAVEL

High-speed travel, as a disruptive technology, has already taken the first step towards reality with the development of the "Hyperloop One" prototype propulsion system. The Hyperloop concept comprises a number of pods suspended on magnets travelling hundreds of kilometres an hour through vacuum tubes. Elon Musk, the founder of Hyperloop, intends to make this a reality before the end of 2020, with the first test site planned for Abu Dhabi. High-speed travel has many benefits, such as solving long-distance travel issues, decreasing carbon pollution and solving the need for urbanisation.

Leaders will have to deal with change quickly and decisively. It is therefore inevitable that high-speed travel, as a disruptive technology, would trigger change as a metaphor for the skills associated with the future-thinking leader. Thinking on your feet and pre-empting potential outcomes in this disruptive environment will become a very useful skill for a leader in dealing with these disruptions in the future.

What is very clear from the development of high-speed travel and medical technologies is that collaboration and negotiation in terms of getting to suitable and sustainable solutions in dealing with modern-day challenges is a unique human quality. The closest machines can come to collaboration (but not negotiation) is through human-initiated digital twinning. Digital twinning enables machines to monitor their own performance data and continuously compare it with that of other machine models of the same specifications. Machines will report any deviances from the digital twining norms in order for humans to make the best decision to mitigate variances in performance. The collaboration of machines is thus artificial and there is no negotiation towards a solution, which is for humans to do. In the end, negotiation and authentic collaboration will play a vital role in the challenges that the 4IR is going to pose. It will require a much more mature approach to leadership than ever before.

SPACE COLONISATION AND EXPLOITATION

Various enterprises are currently exploring space colonisation and exploitation, including SpaceX, Virgin Galactic, Blue Origin and Stratolauch. SpaceX asserts that it will be a pioneer in the field of colonisation and maintain that it will make the human race multiplanetary. On the other hand, Virgin Galactic will promote space tourism from its site in Albuquerque, New Mexico.

Space exploitation planning and design are already very far down the line, and the prospect of space mining and the accommodation of space mining crews is no longer a far-fetched idea. The capability of humans to effectively deal with disruptions in future will become an important skill. Visionary capability, as a skill set, will become more and more important, as will the ability to see opportunities beyond the current day-to-day challenges we are currently facing. Space thinking has never been as relevant as it is now, and has the ability not just to think out of the box, but also to throw away the box and space-think. We believe that, in future, leadership will require much more out-of-your-comfort-zone thinking, while leading others accordingly.

THE WAY FORWARD

Disruptive technologies are varied and complex, and require a very different kind of leader than in the past. The successful adoption by humans and the subsequent implementation of new technological developments implies that previous-century leadership theories and models will not stand up to the leadership skills requirements of the future. The particular differences required of future leaders will become clear in the application of the 4.0D® Leadership Development Model.

SKILLS REQUIRED IN THE 4IR

"It's supposed to be automatic, but
actually you have to push this button."

John Brunner

In 2016, the WEF published an online article written by Alex Gray titled "The 10 skills you need to thrive in the Fourth Industrial Revolution". The First, Second and Third Industrial Revolutions were based on mechanical production equipment, driven by water and steam power, on mass production enabled by the division of labour and the use of electrical energy, and on the use of electronics and information technology (IT) to further automate production.

The ten skills first listed by Gray in 2015 that are required to thrive in the 4IR are shown in comparison to the skills necessary in 2020. These are as follows:

IN 2015	IN 2020
1. Complex problem-solving	1. Complex problem-solving
2. Coordinating with others	2. Critical thinking
3. People management	3. Creativity
4. Critical thinking	4. People management
5. Negotiation	5. Coordinating with others
6. Quality control	6. Emotional intelligence
7. Service orientation	7. Judgement and decision-making
8. Judgement and decision-making	8. Service orientation
9. Active listening	9. Negotiating
10. Creativity	10. Cognitive flexibility

Table 3: Comparison of the skills needed for the 4IR

Gray indicated that, in comparison, more than a third of the skills required in 2015 would have changed in 2020. If one considers a comparison of the skills predicted for the future in Table 3, some of the top 10 skills fell off the list for 2020. The most important shift in skills needed was creativity, which moved from tenth to third position. From the 2020 skills list, it becomes quite clear that a cluster of management- and leadership-related skills now rank in positions 4 to 6. Human interaction has become a vital skill set required for the next industrial revolution.

In 2020, the Crimson Global Academy's website asserted that the top ten jobs in the next decade require certain key skills, and there is a large overlap with the skills mentioned in Table 3.

The five key (human) skills mentioned for future employment are the following:

- Mental elasticity and complex problem-solving
- Critical thinking
- Creativity
- People skills
- Interdisciplinary knowledge

From this, one can derive that people skills continuously form part of the skills set to contribute to successful leadership in the future, despite the ever-increasing influence and role of technology in the workplace. One of the key aspects that form the crux of the 4.0D® Leadership Development Model is the assertion that leadership starts from within an individual.

There are certain skills sets and personal insights associated with being a good leader. This includes understanding one's own capabilities and personal leadership developmental needs.

Prior to 2020, an article published in the South African newspaper, *Beeld,* in January 2017 lists the following as tasks that machines will not be able to do in future.

These skills, ranked in order of importance, are the following:

1. Problem-solving
2. Adaptability
3. Leadership
4. Creativity and innovation
5. Emotional intelligence

Leadership was the third-most important skill needed, but its importance will probably increase exponentially as the revolutions proceed beyond the 4IR. People and – for that matter – future leaders will have to adapt to a new set of skills in order to be successful in the 4IR and beyond. Incorporating and updating new skills as the future progresses will be a very dynamic process, and the ability to respond timeously to the new skills needed to cope in future will become more and more important. A new generation of innovative complex problem-solvers, who also possess people skills, and the quality of leaders with a new mindset, will have to drive the current and future industrial revolutions.

LEADERSHIP CHALLENGES AND THE FUTURE IN THE 4IR AND BEYOND

"The Fourth Industrial Revolution is still in its nascent state. But with the swift pace of change and disruption to business and society, the time to join in is now."

Gary Coleman

In 2017, Sattar Bawany expanded on leaders facing the daunting task of restoring confidence and respect in leadership and business.

The concomitant challenge is to achieve this in the context of increasingly disruptive global economies with high levels of cynicism and mistrust against economic and political circumstances.

Bawany cites Klaus Schwab who asserted that there would be enormous managerial leadership challenges as the impact of technology and the associated disruption will result in an exogenous force over which leaders have little or no control at times. In this regard, he explains that the role of leaders to guide their teams and be mindful of these forces when making business decisions will influence the sustainability of organisations. Leaders must therefore shape the 4IR and direct it toward a future that reflects the organisation's value and success. Leaders must also develop a comprehensive and globally shared view of how technology is reshaping the economic, social, cultural and human environments, thereby affecting the lives of their employees.

Bawany argues that today's leaders and decision makers are too often trapped in traditional, linear thinking, or too absorbed by the multiple crises demanding their attention, to think strategically about the forces of disruption and innovation shaping their organisations' future.

Enterprises must adapt to change by adopting solutions and innovations brought about by disruptive technologies. It will be necessary to extend beyond the current fixed value chains, shifting knowledge away from production points to off-site trans-organisational knowledge hubs and shared services. In this lies the requirement of a leader with a specific set of future skills.

When we consider the interface between technology and people in 4IR organisations, it is clear that a singular set of rules or skills will not be sufficient. It is therefore imperative that relevant skills are identified and that these skills, especially those related to leadership, should be developed accordingly. The challenge with this is to develop a leadership development model that will be multi-contextually relevant and appropriately encompass people and leadership skills ranges.

Our experience in the field of leadership development has played a significant role in the process of developing the 4.0D® Leadership Development Model for the 4IR and beyond. The future of industries and leadership will be completely different. The adoption of various technologies has already caused disruption in industries like mining, banking, financial services, communications, manufacturing, real estate and transportation. It will be futile to think that future leaders will cope with these changes when they are developed on antique models and theories of the previous century.

Here, it is important to note that disruption, although typically associated with negative connotations, denotes the idea of improving or enhancing the status quo in the 4IR.

A 2017 PricewaterhouseCoopers publication stated that technology could be a fundamental success factor for industry. It asserts that we live in a world where "leading practice", rather than "best practice" is the goal. In this vein, rapid advancements in technology, such as robotics, remote operations, drones, machine learning and blockchains, mean that even if innovations are cutting edge today, they might not even exist in five or ten years' time.

The question that arises is how to build that flexibility into a business or capital plan (as well as your workforce) if that business may have a lifespan of 20 to 30 years. In this case, it is evident that there is a fundamental mismatch between the lifecycle of finite assets and the lifecycle of both technologies and digital enablement.

In a 2016 article titled "Leadership challenges of the 4th Industrial Revolution", Howell and Buckup say that leadership is about defining what the future should look like and getting stakeholders not only to share, but also to develop that future together. This notion is at the core of the WEF's 4IR research and the design of its programming. In this regard, it offers a vast array of future analyses and questions. Some of these are the following:

- What happens when the future reveals itself only by blurring the boundaries between the physical, digital and biological?
- Technological change not only forces us to reassess reality, but also to reflect on and reassert our values. Defining the need and importance of values in a new leadership development model is therefore an important part of the adoption of new technology in the 4IR and future revolutions.
- Shaping the impact of technological change, leaders must clarify what matters most, in what balance, and with what trade-offs.

Howell and Buckup state that the key understanding is that technology does not evolve in isolation. As much as it is a product of science and engineering, technology is also a product of values and institutions.

Rather than asking what technology will do to us, we need a shared vision of how it can better benefit economies, societies and ourselves. The challenge is to convince our leaders to collaborate to this end, as the true impact of the 4IR lies in our own hands.

However, as indicated in previous sections, industrial revolution cycles will shorten and it is apt to expand briefly on the world beyond the 4IR.

THE FIFTH INDUSTRIAL REVOLUTION

"The fourth and fifth industrial revolutions will work in parallel, with the 5IR defining the ethics and impact of the technology developed in the 4IR. In the 5IR, we're going to have to have... a chief ethical and humane use officer"

Marc Benioff

Until now, the focus has primarily been on industries in the context of the 4IR. Nevertheless, taking into account the cyclic nature of industrial revolutions, we must prepare ourselves for those to come. The 4IR, with its disruptive technologies, like all political, economic, biological or natural upheavals, will clearly expose inequalities among people. It has therefore been theorised that the 5IR will aim to correct these inequalities.

Briefly, the 5IR will be about advancing humanity in the workplace, and business for profit will transform into business for benefit. Many claim that there are indications that a variety of sectors of the world economy are on the verge of the 5IR.

Presently, the 5IR is conceptual and there is a scramble to determine exactly what this will entail. In 2019, Lindsay and Hudson reviewed various views and opinions on the 5IR. They list them as follows:

- Futurist George Muir argues it will be the AI revolution (although this is pretty much what Industry 4.0 is)

- Member of the European Parliament, Eva Kaili, thinks that it is all to do with the potential of quantum computing (this is also still 4.0)
- Genpact believes that it would be when humans and machines combine in the workplace.

To this end, Gauri and Van Eerden published a piece on the WEF's website in 2019 in which they amplify the significance of the 5IR by highlighting what is referred to as the shift of business to making profit with a wider purpose than before. Similar to the shift from profit to benefit, they assert an increasing tendency of business to change its purpose of profitability for shareholders to the general good of man. One of the reasons for this phenomenon is consumer demand for it. Businesses who respond to these demands will offer sustainably minded brands and offerings that are aware of consumer needs.

In 2020, Gardiner explained that the 5IR would go beyond pure technology and disruption on humanity towards the service of humanity. Furthermore, the 5IR will draw together AI and quantum computing with humans. It simply means that the 5IR is the post-human adaptation embracing the technology epoch, which he describes as humans and machines dancing together, metaphorically. The implication for leadership is a shift towards the "people are our business" adage. While these views may describe a potential future state, they raise the question: Does this really justify a following industrial revolution or is it merely an outcome of humans accepting technology and maturing the interface with technological developments?

Currently, the 5IR is still only conceptual, and while the speculation of how it will manifest continues, the question should really rather shift to what the implications would be for leadership. What is very clear now is that the nature of work, the workplace and industries have changed forever. If organisational and business purposes will shift towards human benefit, the notion of "people are our business" strengthens immensely. This further amplifies the need for a specific leadership development model that would be able to accommodate these various complexities and deal with them accordingly. The proposed 4.0D® Leadership Development Model has at its core the intention to allow the development of leadership skills to cope in our VUCA environment on the one hand, and people as perhaps the most complex entity on the other.

CONCLUDING REMARKS

"Any skilled engineer can take control remotely of any connected 'thing'. Society has not yet realised the incredible scenarios this capability creates."

André Kudelski

The future entails leadership functioning in cyber-physical systems, cloud computing, IoT and cognitive computing that will underlie the mechanisation and modernisation of workplaces. In these contexts, leaders will necessarily have to contend with increasingly complex decision making, while exercising emotional intelligence and simultaneously having impact and the ability to inspire, motivate and deal with this complexity in a volatile, uncertain, complicated and ambiguous world.

This environment will require introspective leaders who continually challenge and develop their analytical abilities and leadership effectiveness more than ever before. One of the main challenges in dealing with the 4IR and beyond is the ability of the leader to make something of the VUCA environment in how they lead their teams while making sense of "chaos".

It is, however, important that each person in a leadership position understands that leadership starts from within. It is important to note that a set of skills pertaining to managing and leading yourself and your teams starts with a clear understanding and insight into members' personal abilities and capabilities in relation to the skills required in the 4IR and beyond.

In addition, leadership adaptive challenges during disruption require novel solutions, but until we discover them, our future readiness will rely upon greater resilience, adaptability and agility. The relevance and applicability of these factors in the context of the whole-leader principle is a central theme we strongly incorporated into the 4.0D® Leadership Development Model.

For enterprises to compete, grow and create jobs, they must ensure that they have access to people who can lead in a world of high-tech innovation and transformative disruption.

Successful leadership development depends on industry's commitment to increase investments in innovation, equip the workforce with relevant skills at all levels and deliver higher-value goods and services successfully traded globally. With the rapid and practically exponential advancement of technology, the need to address leadership development on a wider scale in all industries is more relevant than ever before.

CHAPTER 4:
FORMULATING THE 4.0D® LEADERSHIP DEVELOPMENT MODEL: THE THINKING BEHIND THE THINKING

"Few would argue that our old paradigms need to change, that yesterday's answers will not provide the way forward, and that the trustworthy maps and familiar territories of the past have little use for the territories that beckon. The need to rewrite our maps and create new reference points is as essential as it is urgent".

Keith Coates

INTRODUCTION

This chapter presents the factors that influenced the thinking behind the thinking when it came to designing the 4.0D® Leadership Development Model. In the process of developing the model, certain criteria were set for the new model:

- It needed to be independent of a specific leadership style and approach.
- The model should expand beyond the world of work and people only. It needs to transcend the two-dimensional bi-axial simplistic designs of the past because leadership is more complex than a two-factor approach.

- The model design should meet the leadership requirements and demands of the 4IR and beyond and must address a wide variety of industrial leadership contexts.
- It must entail an eclectic and neutral approach that picks on the best of the best of what current leadership theories have to offer.
- To avoid a very complex and incomprehensible combination of leadership compass points, it should be visually and graphically demonstrable for easy comprehension and understanding of human dynamics.
- It should integrate these human dynamics in a logical and understandable way.
- The most fundamental criteria is for the new leadership development model to have, at its core, the Three-part Mind as it manifests in the affect, behaviour and cognition of the person who fulfils the leadership position.
- Finally, the model must provide and equip leaders with the ability to lead in disruptions in business, whatever the origin, scale and range of the disruption may be.

These design criteria are further guided by the principles of Simon Sinek's Golden Circle, as described in his book, *"Start with why: How great leaders inspire everyone to take action"*, published in 2009. In addition, Sinek's work correlates very highly with the design criteria of the Three-part Mind approach to leadership: affect, behaviour and cognition.

START WITH WHY

"The Golden Circle is an alternative perspective to existing assumptions why some leaders and organisations have achieved such a disproportionate degree of influence."

Simon Sinek

Briefly, Sinek's Golden Circle comprises three circles. The centre circle is the *why*, the second circle is the *how* and the outer circle as the *what*.

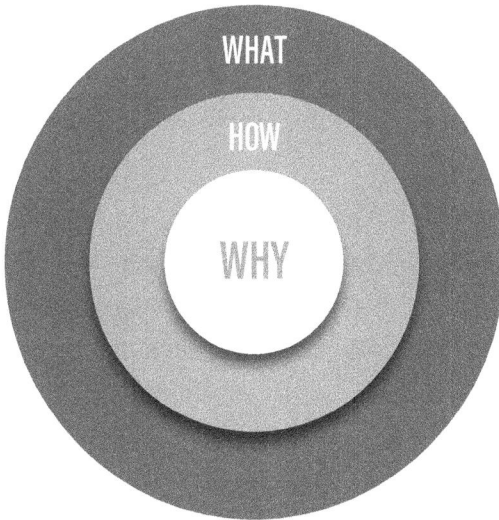

Figure 7: The Golden Circle

Sinek advocates that starting with *why* is more meaningful to get to the *raison d'etre* of an organisation or people pursuing a purpose. This is also the most difficult part to illuminate since it is located in the limbic system, which is the centre of human emotion, and therefore the faculty of language in this part of the brain is limited. In mastering the *why*, the organism (person or organisation) finds meaning and can unlock the inner core of being.

The following actual event illustrates the power of *why* and how it can help clarify things for people and give new perspectives on crucial and key issues.

During a conversation with some senior leaders and executives of a company, its business model of expansion through acquisitions was under discussion. They had to analyse and come up with the reasons *why* their company was doing what it was. The answers varied and ranged from lean and mean, job retention, ability to produce economically, work as safely as possible, and make money. All the answers clearly expanded on the *how* and the *what* they do, but no one articulated the *why*.

Finally, they gave up after quite an extensive discussion. I responded by saying: "You do what you do because you see value where others don't". That was the *why* that drives their business rationale of expanding through the acquisition of other businesses in the same industry. That simple sentence encapsulated the complex whole of an organisation that is worth billions. That is the value of starting with *why*, and we advocate this on a leadership level throughout the development of the 4.0D® Leadership Development Model.

The other two elements of the Golden Circle are the *how* and the *what*. The concept of how usually refers to "doing", the value chain and the methodologies of organisations and people. In this regard, the outer limbic system of the brain (the hippocampus) controls conation or behaviour in biological terms.

The concept of *what* refers to the outcomes, goals, output achievements and resources, infrastructure and equipment needed to reach the targets. There is a strong adaptability and problem-solving element to achieving the *what*: a lot of thinking and adjustments must go into the short-, medium- and long-term goal attainment. Here, the biological structure of the neo-cortex of the human brain is involved. Just like Sinek's Golden Circle, which is an "inside out" model (refer to Figure 7). The 4.0D® Leadership Development Model follows suit in terms of the location of these functions in the structure of the brain.

WEIGHING UP THE OPTIONS: THE ESSENSCE OF THE PILLARS OF THE 4.0D® LEADERSHIP DEVELOPMENT MODEL

By applying the principle of the *why* process, the essence of the 4.0D® Leadership Development Model culminated into four pillars. In order to have influence, the model had to make economic sense and be sufficiently robust to consider future leadership elements. In terms of the criteria presented at the beginning of this chapter, the model had to be enduring and remain useful and sustainable over time (even decades to come), and finally be untarnished by the social dynamics and political contexts of its time.

THE FIRST PILLAR: TRIPLE BOTTOM LINE

"You never change things by fighting the existing reality.
To change something, build a new model that makes the existing
model obsolete."

Buckminster Fuller

The first pillar that shaped our thinking was the triple bottom line. In 1997, Elkington coined the phrase "triple bottom line" in the book *"Cannibals with forks: The triple bottom line of 21st century business"*. This refers to a business approach that covers the financial, environmental and social aspects of businesses. The triple bottom line means Profit, Planet and People (PPP). In the context of sustainability, it is very appropriate in many industries in appreciating business and leadership.

The first stage of the leadership challenge usually starts in the inception phase, during the start-up of a company. This brings the urgency of achieving profit and shareholder wealth into focus.

The second stage of the leadership challenge emerged during the second half of the previous century. It meant taking greater care of the planet and ecosystem health. The emergence of several professional interest groups, some of which maintained a very activist stance concerning organisations' impact on the environment triggered this stage. The most notable of these was Greenpeace.

In the third stage, which emerged towards the end of the previous century, leaders were pushed to develop and demonstrate values with the main aim of addressing the implications of their actions for society as a whole. This stage then marked the advent of corporate social responsibility (CSR) and corporate social investment (CSI).

CSR and CSI were largely shaped by the initial seven and later eight Sullivan principles, which were initially developed to put pressure on the South African government to end apartheid. However, the principles eventually gained wide adoption among US-based corporations. Briefly, the Sullivan principles state: "As a company which endorses the Global

Sullivan Principles, we will respect the law, and as a responsible member of society, we will apply these principles with integrity consistent with the legitimate role of business. We will develop and implement company policies, procedures, training and internal reporting structures to ensure commitment to these principles throughout our organisation. We believe the application of these principles will achieve greater tolerance and better understanding among peoples, and advance the culture of peace."

Moreover, the relevance of the triple bottom line that shaped our thinking is essentially the impact of the 4IR and beyond on the future of business. Whereas organisations nowadays often practice CSR and CSI because it is "the right thing to do", the 4IR and beyond is going to shift the emphasis from *profit* for shareholders to *benefit* for people.

It is also going to expose and make inequality more evident. Just these two shifts pose great challenges for future leaders who must make business work, yet may most likely also face (shareholder) antagonism towards these disruptive shifts.

In 2018, Elkington actually stated that he wanted to recall the notion of the triple bottom line since "...success or failure on sustainability goals cannot be measured only in terms of profit and loss. It must also be measured in terms of the wellbeing of billions of people and the health of our planet, and the sustainability sector's record in moving the needle on those goals has been decidedly mixed. While there have been successes, our climate, water resources, oceans, forests, soil and biodiversity are all increasingly threatened. It is time to either step up – or to get out of the way."

While leaders, and thus corporations of the past, failed on the environmentally safe and low industry impact criteria required by the triple bottom line, the question is whether this really warrants a recall of the concept. As indicated in Chapter 3, the 4IR and beyond actually holds a lot of promise for the betterment of the environment as well, and this may very well support the triple bottom line.

Perhaps environmental neglect may be the result of companies that embraced a variety of leadership development programmes, most of which were based, to some extent, on many of the current leadership theories mostly developed and postulated in the previous century. Those models and theories never focused on anything other than people and work, so this outcome is quite understandable in that context.

THE SECOND PILLAR: FUTURE LEADERSHIP ELEMENTS

"The machine does not isolate man from the great problems of nature, but plunges him more deeply into it."

Antoine de Saint-Exupéry

The second pillar stems from the requirement for key leadership elements needed for the future, stemming from the 4IR and beyond. Clearly, the leadership theories and models offered in Chapter 2 show that not one single leadership theory contains all the answers and solutions for effective leadership. However, there are many well-researched elements of leadership, which, when combined, can be placed into a relevant, yet eclectic leadership development model design.

What is very clear from the impact of the 4IR is that the future of leadership in industry is going to be much different from that which the current traditional hierarchical structures offer. The privilege of rank in an organisational hierarchy that provides the incumbent with leadership status and a leadership "seat" and its associated command and control authority has no future in future industries. Requisite leadership skills are therefore in need of redesign. For leaders to thrive in the 4IR and beyond, current models and theories in many ways do not comprehensively combine elements for the future. For instance, none of these addresses agility as part of its offerings, but agility in leaders has become a necessity. A rapid agility to change was traditionally not a common characteristic of leadership development in most industries. That is perhaps why it is less common among current leadership pacemakers in a wide variety of industries. Nowadays, however, it is common knowledge that great leaders adapt to change the quickest.

The Ethiopian Airlines Flight 301 is a case study for consideration from which valuable leadership lessons can be learnt. The case study clearly illustrates this point as an example of human agility and rapid adaption to change in a highly technical environment.

CASE STUDY 1: ETHIOPIAN AIRLINES FLIGHT 302,
10 MARCH 2019, NEW YORK TIMES

The March 10, 2020 crash of Ethiopian Airlines Flight 302 killed all 157 passengers and crew on the Boeing 737 Max 8 jet. Data has shown significant similarities between the crash and the Lion Air disaster in October 2018, when the same model of plane crashed soon after take-off in Indonesia. As a result, Boeing 737 Max jets worldwide do not fly as the investigations continue. Ethiopian officials say the pilots followed instructions provided by Boeing as per pilot practice very meticulously.

The event

Just two minutes after take-off, the captain of the doomed Ethiopian Airlines Flight 302 said the plane was having problems. Pilots then began having trouble controlling the aircraft.

In the plane's short and fatal flight, pilots initially followed safety procedures recommended by Boeing, performing actions on the emergency checklist, including cutting off electricity to an automatic system that was pushing the nose down. But they were still unable to prevent the jet from crashing, according to an initial report by Ethiopian investigators.

About six minutes after take-off, the plane went into a fatal dive that killed all 157 people on board the aircraft. Eighteen Ethiopian and international investigators and information from the jet's flight data recorder and cockpit voice recorder were involved in the crash investigation. The investigators' initial report was released several hours after a news conference held by Ethiopia's Minister of Transportation.

The data showed that shortly after lift-off, a crucial sensor that measures the angle that the plane is moving through the air began fluctuating wildly on the pilot's side, falsely indicating that the plane was close to stalling.

The sensor, one of two sensors on the plane's nose, began giving readings nearly 60 degrees different from those of its counterpart.

About a minute and a half after take-off, after the pilots had performed routine tasks like retracting flaps on the wings, the false reading appears to have set off an automated system known as the manoeuvring characteristics augmentation system (MCAS), the black box data shows. The MCAS design is to prevent stall, and actually began to push the nose of the craft down.

A faulty sensor

Moments after take-off, one of two crucial sensors that measure the plane's angle of attack diverged wildly, eventually triggering an automated system that pushed down the nose of the plane. The pilots countered that by pushing electrical switches on their control wheels that adjusted the angle of stabilisers on the tail of the plane. About five seconds after the pilots tried to right the plane, MCAS again engaged, moving the stabilisers to a dangerous angle in another nose-down action.

The pilots pushed the electrical switches again. Then, the report says, they followed the emergency checklist and disabled the entire stabiliser's electrical system, using the so-called stabiliser trim cut out. "The first officer called out "stab trim cut out" twice," the report says. "The captain agreed and the first officer confirmed the stab trim cut out."

Although that move disabled the MCAS, it also forced the crew to control the stabilisers manually with wheels at their feet – a physically difficult task on a plane moving at high speed.

A little under four minutes after take-off, the first officer said the manual method "is not working." Soon after, the black box data indicates, the crew turned electricity back on and tried twice more to move the stabilisers by hitting the switches. But once they turned the electricity back on, MCAS engaged again, putting the plane into a dive from which it would not recover.

The crash of Ethiopian Airlines Flight 302 on March 10 followed the unrecoverable nose-dive almost five months earlier of another jet of the same model, a Boeing 737 Max 8, in Indonesia. Indonesian investigators have implicated MCAS in that disaster, in which the plane's computer system appeared to override pilot directions based on faulty data.

"These guys are executing the checklist," Dennis Tajer, a spokesperson for the American Airlines pilot union, said of the Ethiopian pilots after reviewing the report. "They were identifying the problem and taking swift action."

The initial findings are likely to heighten scrutiny of the Max 8, Boeing's newest and top-selling generation of jets. Since the Ethiopian Airlines crash, airlines worldwide have grounded their Max 8 fleets, amid concerns over the apparent propensity of MCAS to malfunction when fed erroneous data.

Ethiopian authorities portrayed the pilots of the plane in a positive light. Dagmawit Moges, Ethiopia's Minister of Transportation said that the flight crew repeatedly followed procedures recommended by the plane's manufacturer, "but was not able to control the aircraft."

Both 737 Max 8 jets crashed at maximum speed minutes after take-off in clear weather, following roller-coaster trajectories that hinted at desperate struggles by pilots to control planes seemingly immune to their interventions. In a statement Boeing's Chief Executive, Dennis A. Muilenburg, said that the company was "confident in the fundamental safety of the 737 Max 8." Boeing has said it plans to release a software update to MCAS soon, along with increased pilot training for the 737 Max 8 planes.

"This update, along with the associated training and additional educational material that pilots want in the wake of these accidents, will eliminate the possibility of unintended MCAS activation and prevent an MCAS-related accident from ever happening again," Muilenburg said.

While Case Study 1 clearly illustrates many skills, such as identifying problems and seemingly complex decision making, the plane nevertheless flew into the ground at several hundred kilometres per hour. One question that arises if one considers the skills listed in the previous chapter is: "Since this crash was in a highly technologically advanced 4IR environment, surely applying these skills should have saved the situation?"

The answer lies in the fact that complex situations require complex combinations of skills. In this case, a combination of complex problem solving, creativity, critical thinking, judgment, decision making and cognitive flexibility was not evident. The root cause most likely lay in the procedural elements of the aviation industry in which original equipment manufacturers (OEM) manuals prescribe precise procedures and sequential actions for pilots. These pilots were not flexible and did not adapt to the feedback from the faulty equipment.

In this context, consider Case Study 2 below.

CASE STUDY 2: US AIRWAYS FLIGHT 1549,
WIKIPEDIA, THE FREE ENCYCLOPAEDIA

On January 15, 2009, US Airways Flight 1549 with call sign Cactus 1549 was scheduled to fly from New York City's LaGuardia Airport (LGA) to Charlotte Douglas (CLT), with direct onward service to Seattle-Tacoma International Airport. The aircraft was an Airbus A320-214 powered by two GE Aviation/ Snecma-designed CFM56-5B4/P turbofan engines.

The pilot in command was 57-year-old Chesley B. Sullenberger, a former fighter pilot who had been an airline pilot since leaving the US Air Force in 1980. At the time, he had logged 19 663 total flight hours, including 4 765 in an A320. He was also a glider pilot and expert on aviation safety. First officer Jeffrey B. Skiles, 49, had accrued 15 643 career flight hours, but this was his first Airbus A320 assignment since qualifying to fly it. There were 150 passengers and three flight attendants on board.

After take-off, the plane struck a flock of Canadian geese at an altitude of 2 818 feet (859 m) just north-northwest of LaGuardia Airport. The passengers and crew heard very loud bangs and saw flames from the engines, followed by silence and an odour of fuel.

Realising that both engines had shut down, Sullenberger took control while Skiles worked the checklist for engine restart. The aircraft slowed but continued to climb for a further 19 seconds, reaching about 3 060 feet (930 m) at an airspeed of about 185 knots (343 km/h; 213 mph), then began a glide descent, accelerating to 210 knots (390 km/h; 240 mph), and rapidly descended through 1 650 feet (500 m).

Sullenberger radioed a mayday call to New York Terminal Radar Approach Control (TRACON): "... this is Cactus 1539 [sic – correct call sign was Cactus 1549], hit birds. We've lost thrust on both engines. We're turning back towards LaGuardia." Air traffic controller Patrick Harten told LaGuardia's tower to hold all departures, and directed Sullenberger back to Runway 13.

Sullenberger responded, "Unable".

Sullenberger asked controllers for landing options in New Jersey, mentioning Teterboro Airport. Air traffic control gave permission for landing on Teterboro's Runway 1.

Sullenberger responded: "We can't do it ... We're gonna be in the Hudson".

The aircraft passed less than 900 feet (270 m) above the George Washington Bridge. Sullenberger commanded over the cabin address system, "Brace for impact" and the flight attendants relayed the command to passengers.

Meanwhile, air traffic controllers asked the Coast Guard to caution vessels in the Hudson and ask them to prepare to assist with rescue.

About ninety seconds later, the plane made an unpowered ditching, descending southwards at about 125 knots (230 km/h; 140 mph) into the middle of the North River section of the Hudson tidal estuary on the New York side of the state line.

Flight attendants compared the ditching to a "hard landing" with "one impact, no bounce, and then a gradual deceleration." The ebb tide then began to take the plane southward.

Sullenberger opened the cockpit door and ordered evacuation. The crew began evacuating the passengers through the four overwing window exits and into an inflatable slide from the front right passenger door (the front left slide failed to operate, so the manual inflation handle was pulled). A panicked passenger opened a rear door, which a flight attendant was unable to reseal. Water was also entering a hole in the fuselage and through cargo doors that had come open, so as the water rose, the attendant urged passengers to move forward by climbing over seats. One passenger was in a wheelchair. Finally, Sullenberger walked the cabin twice to confirm it was empty.

Many craft descended upon the floating airliner and all passengers and crew were successfully taken ashore alive.

Because the plane was assembled in France, the European Aviation Safety Agency (the European counterpart of the FAA) and the Bureau d'Enquêtes et d'Analyses pour la Sécurité de l'Aviation Civile (the French counterpart of the NTSB) joined the investigation, with technical assistance from Airbus and GE Aviation/Snecma, respectively the manufacturers of the airframe and the engines.

The NTSB used flight simulators to test the possibility that the flight could have returned safely to LaGuardia or diverted to Teterboro; only seven of the 13 simulated returns to La Guardia succeeded, and only one of the two to Teterboro.

Furthermore, the NTSB report called these simulations unrealistic: "The immediate turn made by the pilots during the simulations did not reflect or account for real-world considerations." A further simulation, conducted with the pilot delayed by 35 seconds, crashed. In testimony before the NTSB, Sullenberger maintained that there had been no time to bring the plane to any airport, and that attempting to do so would likely have killed those on board and more on the ground.

There was a lot of criticism against Sullenberger for not following the checklist for dual engine failure as contained within the procedure and flight manuals.

The Board, after much deliberation and critique of Sullenberger's decision, ultimately ruled that Sullenberger had made the correct decision.

Their reasoning was that the checklists for dual-engine failure are designed for higher altitudes when pilots have more time to deal with the situation. The simulations showed that the plane might have just barely made it back to LaGuardia, those scenarios assumed an instant decision to do so, with no time allowed for assessing the situation.

Author and pilot William Langewiesche asserted that insufficient credit was given to the A320's fly-by-wire design, by which the pilot uses a side-stick to make control inputs to the flight control computers.

The computers then impose adjustments and limits of their own to keep the plane stable, which the pilot cannot override even in an emergency. This design allowed the pilots of Flight 1549 to concentrate on engine restart and deciding the course, without the burden of manually adjusting the glidepath to reduce the plane's rate of descent. However, Sullenberger said that these computer-imposed limits also prevented him from achieving the optimum landing flare for the ditching, which would have softened the impact.

Most industries have traditionally developed and entrenched what is known as a "command and control culture". In aviation, the captain is the supreme commander of the aircraft. In Case Study 2, Captain Sullenburg indeed asserted his command, but he made extraordinary decisions that veered off from all conventional airline industry protocols.

In the case of Ethiopian Airline crash, the pilots followed technology faultlessly throughout the whole event, but failed to realise that a faulty sensor had caused the roller-coaster ride. Had they done so, perhaps they could have exercised sufficient human intervention to save the plane or the passengers.

In the case of US1549, Sullenberger was able to assert human decision making, complex problem solving and a sense of creativity, despite the immediate pressure and the airline's conventional standard emergency protocol. That is the kind of leader needed for the 4IR and beyond.

THE THIRD PILLAR: LEADERSHIP STYLE

"For those of you who really want to give critical thought to your unique leadership style and foster genuine followership, learn from what's out there and weave it into something meaningful and authentic."

Stacy Feiner

Authors such as Schultz and Bezuidenhout ungroup the various leadership clusters and theories into a number of styles, ranging from bottom-up leadership, to transformational leadership, charismatic leadership, authentic leadership and transactional leadership, but they fail to include servant leadership, as postulated by Blanchard and Hodges a number of years earlier. In analysing the various personality traits of each style, Schultz and Bezuidenhout clearly follow the path of Trait Theory leadership.

Although these styles and style-specific descriptors come in very handy to describe leadership behaviour, they do not essentially address the fundamentals of leadership. The main reason for this is that a leadership style is an outcome of the function of other human dynamics embedded in the intrapersonal make-up and composition of an individual.

Future leadership requirements tend to indicate the need for a new Leadership Development Model as a point of departure for formulating a leadership approach.

This needs to be independent of a specific leadership style and approach to work and people only – it needs to transcend the bi-axial designs of the past.

There is currently a plethora of programmes in leadership development that focus on a variety of factors that influence leadership, such as emotional intelligence and other motivational aspects related to leaders with visionary thinking, as offered by Schultz and Bezuidenhout. On the other hand, Nicholls describes a three-tier leadership approach that essentially attempts to integrate the three basic intrapersonal dynamics of individuals: the head, which relates to strategic leadership; the heart, which implies inspirational leaders; and the hands, which encompasses behaviour and actions in the task execution of the supervisory leader.

Furthermore, there was a definite trend in the latter part of the previous century to focus on leadership styles as a suitable way to analyse how leaders function in organisations.

In his "12 different types of leadership styles", Ahmed Raza lists the following:

- Autocratic leadership
- Democratic leadership
- Strategic leadership
- Transformational leadership
- Team leadership
- Cross-cultural leadership
- Facilitative leadership
- Laissez-faire leadership
- Transactional leadership
- Coaching leadership
- Charismatic leadership
- Visionary leadership

These leadership styles are usually posited as leadership solutions for organisations. The most notable recent leadership style is Goulston's 'Heartfelt' leadership, which focuses mainly on emotional connectivity between leaders and followers in the form of caring and trust.

All of the above approaches and theories of leadership are very valid and, until now, served leadership (to a large extent) very well. What is very evident in all these approaches is the lack of integration of leadership theories and models, and leadership styles. This may perhaps be the core element missing to bind these leadership theories and the various styles together. The lack of an integrated leadership development model creates approaches towards leadership that are too diverse and do not address future requisite leadership in a fitting manner.

With such diverse leadership styles, the last thing one needs is to yet again replicate or offer just another inappropriate model that will clutter the leadership landscape even more.

The *why* here, was not to follow the style path, but rather develop a leadership development model that is not style dependant or related. In this new approach, style is a personal outcome of the SELF (we will elaborate on this in Chapter 5). In addition, leadership style, as such, is not the route to take in that context. Nicholls's three-tier leadership approach (head, hands and heart) is of value, but we deliberately "de-styled" it by linking it to its biological origins. This was the *why* catalyst in the new approach that led to the fourth factor that guides the new thinking: the very stable factor of biology, which acts as the source of human dynamics that informs all the social sciences.

THE FOURTH PILLAR: STABILITY OVER TIME FACTORS

"No social stability without individual stability. "

Aldous Huxley

Existing leadership theories are essentially products of the contextual thinking and social dynamic influences during their postulation periods. These range from political events, socio-economics, national and international politics and cultural influences, which literally changed from decade to decade, especially in the latter part of the 20th century.

The fourth pillar entails the notion to pursue an alternative option and formulate a model that is free of current, past or possible future socio-dynamic influences that change from time to time. This thus eliminates current theories and models, since they stem from that context.

We are, however, of the opinion that there are elements of these theories that have merit and may still contribute towards a leadership development model for the future. The question was how to do it and which elements to select in a coherent and rational way that makes sense. In addition, it should help to build a model to describe leadership for the future comprehensively. The intention was also to strive towards the development of a leadership development model that would be understandable and "application friendly".

In view of this, the next question that arose was "How can one find or design 'stability over time' in a model if human factors of leadership research are subject to influence by rapid changes in the socio-dynamic domain?"

The answer lies in anatomy and biology. It was not in research on psychology, anthropology, sociology or any of the social sciences. These are too socio-dynamically sensitive. Biology is not.

An example here is the cultural anthropological work of Margaret Mead. Her research clearly illustrates the socio-dynamics of a certain era and that subjectivity stemming from personal life experiences can lead to research bias. Influenced by her first affair with a man with very conservative ideas about marriage and a woman's role in life, she expended all her research focus in this direction. Mead researched gender consciousness in the South Pacific, particularly in Samoa, which focused on attitudes towards sex among younger Samoan women. Her research methodology comprised qualitative interviews as a vehicle to data gathering.

One of her main findings was the relatively relaxed and uninhibited attitude towards sex and sexuality in Samoa. She used this as a guide to broaden the conventions of the Western cultural traditions through her publications.

She largely influenced the attitudes of Western society, specifically America, and this played a huge part in the sexual revolution if the 1960's and the lifestyle of the hippies. Her work understandably drew a lot of criticism, particularly from Derek Freeman, who claimed that she was misled by the young women he re-interviewed a number of years later. Despite Freeman's antagonism, Mead's work made an impact. However, it also has a shelf life, and many of her findings and conclusions are not valid in the world of today. In the context of the dynamics behind Mead's work, it is reasonable to assume that most social research is vulnerable to bias, despite research designs to control for this.

In contrast to time- and context-bound social research, the path to pursue in building a leadership development model based on biology is because human anatomy has not changed much in centuries. Perhaps what has changed dramatically in recent times is man's ability and speed to create, absorb and process knowledge. To master that, humans do not need a structurally changed brain or anatomy. They just have to train their brains to increase information processing and absorption. Some records claim that the *New York Times* contains more information in the Sunday edition than the knowledge a person could have gathered in a lifetime in the 1800's.

The New Zealand academic, James Flynn, asserts that people are, in fact, getting cleverer. This is known as "the Flynn Effect". He bases this assertion on the fact that, all over the world, people's IQs measure higher nowadays than in the past. Since IQ is purely a cognitive process, it is questionable whether people with high IQs make good leaders. What is of importance now is that intelligence or cognition certainly plays a role, but in conjunction with conation (behaviour) and affect (emotion), as discussed in the third pillar of leadership. The conclusion was that the answer lies in biology, thus yielding the fourth pillar.

THE THREE-PART MIND

"Biology gives you a brain. Life turns it into a mind."

Jeffrey Eugenides

In line with this, we support the notion of Kolbe's Three-part Mind, which really comes from the German psychology of the 18th century. However, it did not remain there, as it received recognition from the Association of Psychologists of the 19th century in Scotland, England and America.

The Three-part Mind has been alluded to elsewhere as affect, behaviour and cognition. The root of the Three-part Mind lies in the biological structure of the human brain.

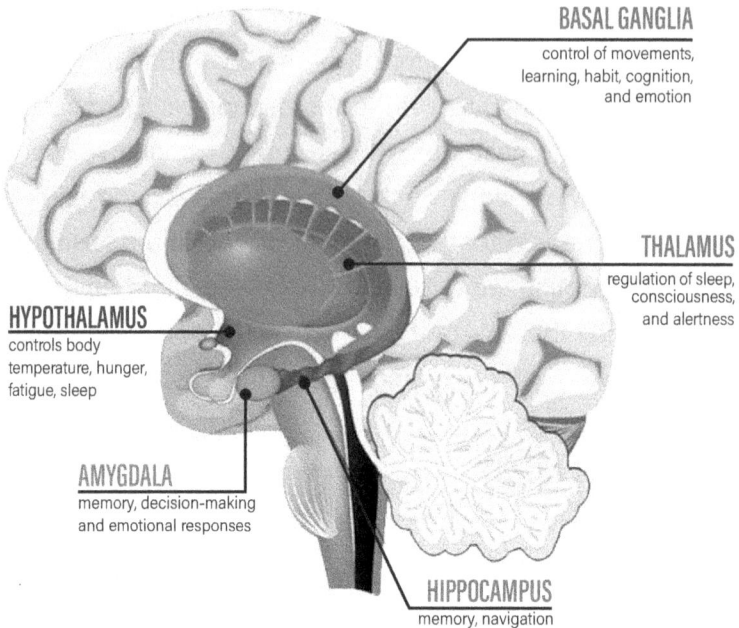

Figure 8: The human brain

As illustrated in Figure 8, the amygdala is the part of the limbic system of the brain that controls the seat for affect – emotional responses. The hippocampus controls behaviour expressed and navigation i.e. deliberate movement. Cognition (intellectual functioning) is located in the very well-known neo-cortex of the brain (the grey shaded area).

LIMBIC SYSTEM AND EMOTIONS

The limbic system is a group of interconnected structures located in the centre of the brain. It is largely responsible for human beings' emotional responses. The following parts of the limbic system are generally associated with and directly centred on emotions:

- **Hypothalamus:** In addition to controlling emotional responses, the hypothalamus is also involved in sexual responses, hormone release and regulating body temperature.

- **Amygdala**: The amygdala helps coordinate responses to things in a person's environment, especially those that trigger an emotional response. This structure plays an important role in fear and anger.
- **Limbic cortex:** This part contains two structures: the cingulate gyrus and the parahippocampal gyrus. Together, they influence and control mood, motivation and judgement.

HIPPOCAMPUS AND BEHAVIOUR

The hippocampus plays a vital role in human behaviour that is both flexible and goal-directed. It helps people form and reconstruct relational memory and orientation in the context of navigation – literally where to go and what to do, in conjunction with a flexible cognition and social behaviour.

Studies of the hippocampus indicate that damage to it will impair the flexible use of information and cause maladaptive behaviour. This maladaptive behaviour may take many forms. One study showed that damage to the hippocampus often make animals hyperactive. Another animal study observed reduced learning ability to inhibit previously learnt responses. The hippocampus also acts as the evaluation hub for behavioural inhibition and obsessional thinking.

NEOCORTEX AND COGNITION

The neocortex is the characteristic of mammalian brains and the most diversified functioning part of humans. While it has different sub-units and each performs a distinct function, it is the main seat for cognition and cognitive functioning. The neo part is the newest part of the cerebral cortex.

A damaged neocortex will cause one's cognitive ability to be adversely impaired. Cognitive functions mean the following:

- Sensory perception
- Spatial reasoning
- Conscious thought
- Generating motor commands
- Neuronal computations of attention
- Episodic memory
- Complex language processing
- Social and emotional processing
- Sleep, memory and learning processes
- Semantic memories
- Instrumental conditioning
- Transmit sensory information

Cognition is the most common and well-known element of the Three-part Mind. Most people, in everyday functioning, are in cognitive mode and are not very aware of the emotional and conative (behavioural) elements. Those people that have mastered the ability to create synergy and balance between the three elements of the Three-part Mind are generally better adapted to deal with life's demands and leadership. In the 4.0D® Leadership Development Model, we have relabelled the Three-Part Mind as *SELF* to create a collective concept from where leadership begins.

CONCLUDING REMARKS

In understanding the essence of the 4.0D® Leadership Development Model and the four pillars on which the design of the model is based, it should be borne in mind that, while the four pillars are presented separately, they relate to each other and there are mutual influences between them.

The triple bottom line is the economic foundation of leadership in industries. The range of leadership focus should span and incorporate people and the environment (planet), which must transcend profit as the only motive for business. Leaders of the future will have to drive business for the benefit of people and the environment as well.

A development model for leadership should make provision for individuality and the uniqueness of individuals. Therefore, it should not prescribe a particular leadership style – this will develop according to a person's personality, experience and preferences. Its design should be that leadership is sustainable over time, and should not be a product of a specific time context.

The structure of the brain forms the foundation of sustainable leadership. The three core aspects of affect, behaviour and cognition therefore serve as the foundation in the construction of the 4.0D® Leadership Development Model.

CHAPTER 5:
THE 4.0D® LEADERSHIP DEVELOPMENT MODEL

"The challenge of leadership is to be strong, but not rude; be kind, but not weak; be bold, but not bully; be thoughtful, but not lazy; be humble, but not timid; be proud, but not arrogant; have humour, but without folly."

Jim Rohn

INTRODUCTION

The 4.0D® Leadership Development Model design is an impartial leadership development model that integrates the most relevant leadership dimensions for the future from a number of theories of the past in a cohesive, yet unique way. It has an eclectic design and approach and does not prescribe any particular leadership style. In fact, in the context of this model, individuals are encouraged to develop their own leadership styles according to their own personality frameworks. The model is multidimensional and expands beyond the world of work and people. It links leadership in future contexts and integrates various, up to now isolated, elements in a cohesive manner.

The 4.0D® Leadership Development Model encompasses the required leadership skills that arise from the challenges faced by people in leadership positions in the 4IR. Besides reference to the 4IR or Industry

4.0, the 4.0 in the title of the model also refers to the four main dimensions of the model: SELF, WORK, PEOPLE and IMPACT. These four dimensions are the panels of the model.

In constructing the model, the panels and elements were combined visually in such a way that their interactive dynamics can be clearly illustrated and understood. The design that suited the various element combinations transpired to be in the form of a tetrahedron with four aquiline triangles and six straight lines along the edges of the model's shape. Figure 9 illustrates the tetrahedron shape with the four vertex points of the model labelled Affect, Behaviour, Cognition and Direction.

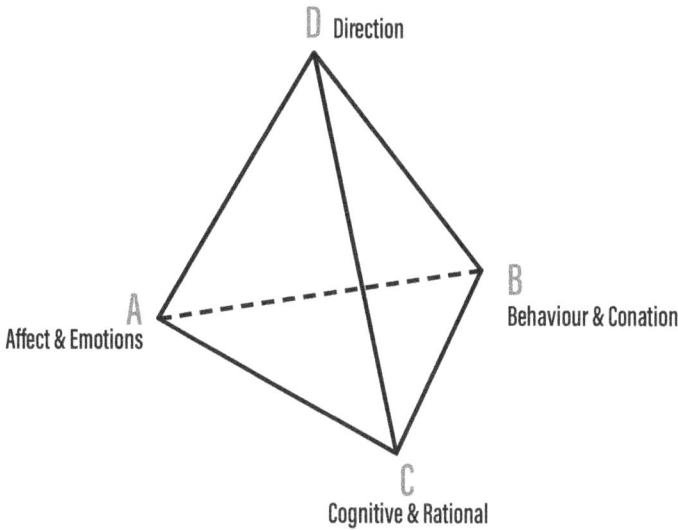

Figure 9: The tetrahedron shape of the model with its four vertex points

The tetrahedron shape integrates the various anatomical structures or parts of leadership into a single model with the three lines of the bottom triangle referred to as action lines.

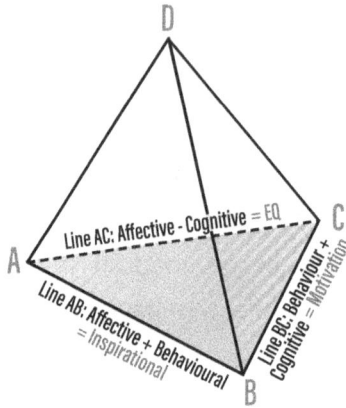

Figure 10: The tetrahedron shape of the model with the base action lines

The Apex (Point D) connects to the base triangle with the directional support lines.

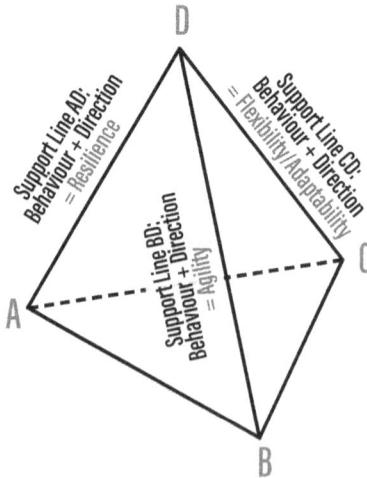

Figure 11: The tetrahedron shape of the model with the directional support lines

The action and directional support lines of the model, together with each of the four vertex points or corners of the triangles, represent the anatomy of leadership. The three major aspects of the 4.0D® Leadership Development Model are therefore the following:

- The tetrahedron shape with the four vertex points: affect, behaviour, cognition and direction (Figure 9)
- The action lines connecting the three points (A, B and C) of the base of the tetrahedron (Figure 10)
- The directional support lines rising from the three base points to the Apex (Figure 11)

THE DIMENSIONS AND ELEMENTS OF THE 4.0D® LEADERSHIP DEVELOPMENT MODEL

THE FIRST DIMENSION: THE BASE – WHERE LEADERSHIP BEGINS (THE SELF)

"I think self-awareness is probably the most important thing towards being a champion."

Billie Jean King

Unlike other leadership theories, the 4.0D® Leadership Development Model focuses rather intensely on the individual who needs to don the mantle of leadership.

We firmly believe that the fundamental point of departure is not only what you do to be a leader. Nor is it the feelings people may entertain from time to time. Leadership is most certainly also not the occasional behaviour that people need to demonstrate at certain times or situations. In essence, leadership starts with the individual himself or herself.

This SELF must reliably represent *all* facets of a human being all the time in an authentic and balanced manner. This constitutes the intra- and interpersonal dimensions of the leader. The basic components of any individual's SELF lie within the biological triad of the brain and its subsequent psychological outflows and human dynamics in the Three-part Mind: Cognition, Affect and Conation. Heightened awareness of this triad simply means increased self-awareness and self-insight.

While we start with Affect in presenting the elements of the SELF in the following section, it should be noted that Affective states are not a series of static processes that, once the person reaches a certain level of maturity, crystallise and become set. Affect, like cognition and conation, will change over an individual's life span during that individual's life journey. This means that the three components of the SELF, as they develop and transform, can contribute to the expansion and growth of the SELF (and thus the base).

Elements of the SELF (the base)
- **Affect & Emotion**: Affective states are a psychosocial construct and the affect refers to the emotional functioning of the individual that usually "kicks in" before the cognitive process becomes active.
- It comprises three basic dimensions:
  - **Valence:** Emotional valence refers to the consequent emotions elicited by a certain situation, as well as emotion-eliciting

circumstances. These are subjective feelings, affect-based attitudes that directly or indirectly relate to the actual situation. It is subject to the individual's emotional state and wellbeing.

- **Arousal:** This physiological response occurs often as a subconscious reaction to the affective interpretation of a stimulus and has a scaled result or control mechanism that varies from extreme arousal on the one hand to complete immobilisation on the other.
- **Motivational Intensity:** In 2013, Gable and Harmon-Jones found that affective states with high motivational intensity cause a narrow attentional scope (a focused state with the goal of zooming in on the goal or object needed or desired). Affective states with low motivational intensity cause relatively broad attentional scope (a relaxed state in which the scope broadens to seek new opportunities).

- **Cognition & Rational:** This relates to intellectual functioning. In the early 2000's, Anderson and Krathwohl revised their taxonomy, first described by the educational psychology of the 1950's. The taxonomy of the cognitive domain comprises the following, in order of increasing complexity:
  - **Remembering:** This aspect constitutes recognition and recalling knowledge from memory: remembering to recite previously learnt information and to produce or retrieve definitions, facts or lists from memory.
  - **Understanding:** This entails constructing meaning from a variety of functions such as written or graphic messages; including activities like interpreting, exemplifying, classifying, summarising, inferring, comparing or explaining.
  - **Applying:** This entails executing or implementing using a specific procedure. This step implies situations of using learnt materials and

content through processes like models, presentations, interviews or simulations.

- **Analysing:** This involves separating information or concepts into parts to determine how various parts relate or interrelate to one another, or how the parts relate to an overall structure or purpose: to differentiate, organise and attribute, as well as an ability to distinguish between various parts or components, make up the mental actions of this function.

- **Evaluating:** This means that judgment is based on criteria and standards by checking and critical analyses. Reports and critiques, recommendations and reports are examples of outcomes to demonstrate the processes of evaluation. In this taxonomy, evaluating comes before creating. Evaluation is precursory behaviour to creating something.

- **Creating:** This is the ability to group elements to form a coherent or functional unit (or whole). It entails reorganising elements into new patterns or structures by generating a plan, or producing a way forward. It requires people either to put parts together in a new way, or to synthesise it into a new and different form or product. This process is the highest order of cognition and the most difficult mental function in the new taxonomy.

- **Conation & Behaviour:** Conation is the third faculty of the mind and is the result of the interactive working of the cognitive and affect, and conation therefore represents the subsequent behaviour (how affect and cognition translate into the individual's behaviour). Whereas Affect and Cognition drive their own domains, neither of them drive action on how to turn ideas into results. Looking at a problem in a smart way may seem to be effective cognitive functioning and behaviour, but it falls short of the methods of doing. For instance, an individual will perhaps be highly effective in problem analyses, but in the absence of conation, nothing will happen to solve the problem. Conation is that vehicle and becomes tangible through volition. Conation is critical if an individual is to engage successfully in self-direction and self-regulation. The Ethiopian Airline case study illustrates this point clearly. The pilot detected the problem accurately, but could not or did not solve it, so the airliner crashed. Despite recognition as far back as the times of Aristotle, conation has never really enjoyed the same attention as cognition and affect, notwithstanding its recognition as the third element of Kolbe's Three-part Mind approach. In the 4.0D® Leadership Development Model, we certainly recognise its status as a vital leg of the SELF.

A fundamental rule

A fundamental principle of the SELF dimension of the 4.0D® Leadership Development Model is that the interactive "balance" between Affect, Conation (Behaviour) and Cognition (the A-B-C) must ideally be perfect (or at least strive to strike a balance towards the triad in synergy and balance). Here we refer to the construct of congruence: the A-B-C relationship between and functioning must be in balance and meet the criteria of a congruent triangle, i.e. three equal sides and three equal angles.

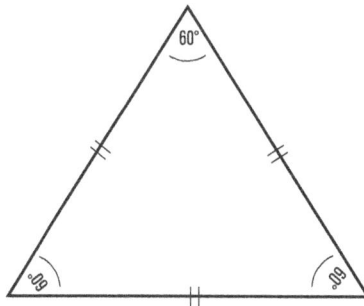

Figure 12: The congruent triangle

Hence, the assertion that leadership starts with the SELF (the base of the model) requires a sound platform.

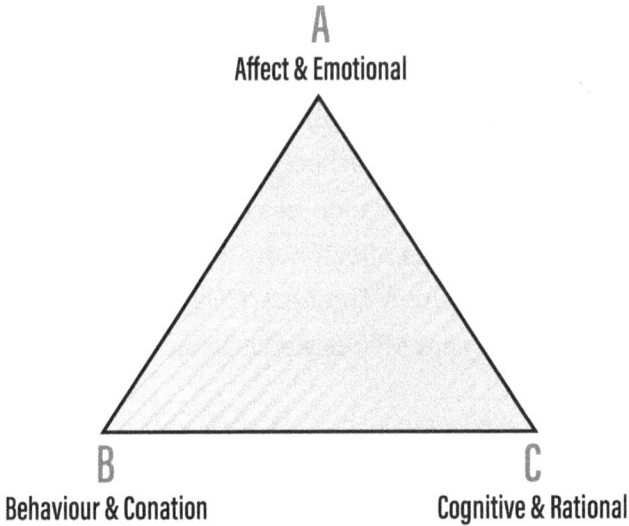

Figure 13: The base and its three points of the SELF

In the 4.0D® Leadership Development Model, the point of departure is to do the following:

- Attain an increased awareness and insight into one's own Affect & Emotional, Conation & Behaviour and Cognition & Rational through the application and developmental exposures inherent in the 4.0D® Leadership Development Model.
- Strive and work towards achieving a balance between the three elements in order to attain full congruency status.

This is most probably the hardest challenge in leadership mastery. One often encounters people who are unable to do this spontaneously.

This is because they are unaware of how or what to do to explore their own emotions. However, a balance is necessary to establish a secure leadership foundation. If this triangle is not congruent, the tetrahedron may become unstable because of imbalances in the base. If the base, as the foundation, becomes unstable, it is likely that the imbalance will lead to leadership failure. Various ways to achieve insight into and create a balance between one's own behaviour, cognition and emotions must form part of the development journey. Some of these are introspection, 360° feedback discussions, reflective exercises, as well as formative assessments, such as the online 4.0D® Leadership Assessment Protocol mentioned in the latter part of this chapter.

Connecting the SELF elements of the base: Dynamic Action lines
The base components do not function in isolation, but the triad of the SELF (A, B and C) interact with each other. An acceptable SELF implies a balanced triangle, meaning a congruent condition. Any incongruence implies an imbalance. Once an affected component has been detected in the base, intervention should be initiated to restore the balance and congruency.

While we deal with these dynamic action lines separately in the sections to follow, it would be purely for comprehension of the model. The dynamic action lines are actually inseparable and represent the "Gestalt" (the whole as the sum of its parts) of the human dynamics as it emanates from the interactive energies between A, B and C. These action lines can be very complex. What the model offers is a distillation of each in terms of the core and basic elements.

Insight into the action lines enables individuals to start getting it right. Eventually, with practise and application of the basic elements, people will become subconsciously competent and proficient. Figure 14 illustrates the SELF as the base with the interactive action lines between the three triangular elements of the SELF.

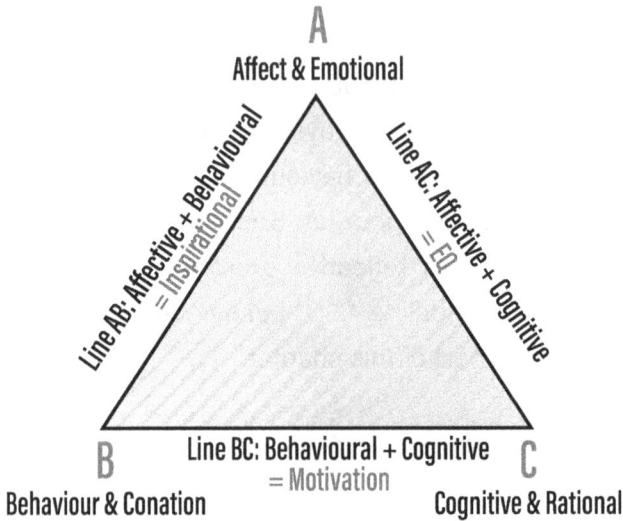

Figure 14: The SELF as the base with the interactive action lines

The A-B Line: The interaction of the Affect with Behaviour to effect Inspiration

"The best way to find yourself is to lose yourself in the service of others."

Mahatma Gandhi

People usually remember and will follow leaders if they offer something that is worthwhile. In addition, many people assert that inspiration is that unique element that not only makes them follow leaders, but believe in them. We thus imply that an important dimension of leadership is the ability to have an impact in an array of settings, be that on individuals, groups, organisations and even communities or countries.

The fundamental element of impact is to do, model and advocate inspirational things and messages. The outcome

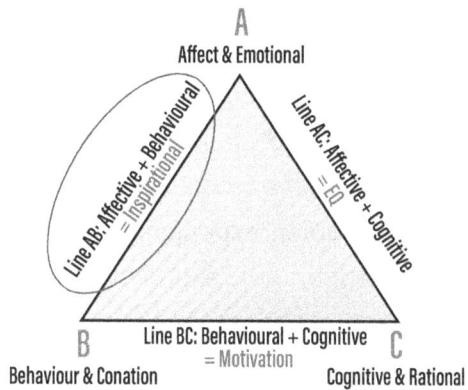

A
Affect & Emotional

Line AB: Affective + Behavioural = Inspirational

Line AC: Affective + Cognitive = EQ

B
Behaviour & Conation

Line BC: Behavioural + Cognitive = Motivation

C
Cognitive & Rational

of this interaction is widely seen in the domain of the transformational and charismatic leadership styles. The central leadership behavioural theme is the development of an ability to inspire, and that should be the catalyst towards having an impact.

Leaders who have impact typically believe in what they stand for and they believe in the vision they hold on their personal journeys, whether it is personal or vocational. Inspiration comes in many forms. Steve Jobs, for instance, linked it to certain personal "life rules". Of these, the following have direct bearing on inspiration in the context of the 4.0D® Leadership Development Model:

- **Do what you love:** People who are in jobs they hate will hardly find inspiration in their jobs. Leaders are the people in organisations that let others find that one thing in what they do to love their jobs. It is not always in the day-to-day activities, but in the achievement and results of what they do and what they achieve. To create meaning for others is to inspire.
- **Put a dent in the universe:** If people have a vision, they will feel differently about what they are doing. Jobs attracted like-minded

people who shared his vision. They turned his ideas into world-changing innovations.

- **Kickstart your brain:** Rethink your thinking. Innovation needs creativity, and for Jobs, creativity was about connecting things. He believed that a broad set of experiences broadened an understanding of the human experience. To inspire people, work on your general knowledge, get experience or knowledge in adventurous and interesting things and share it.
- **Master the message:** Everybody has a story to tell, but to make it inspirational; it should contain a lesson, meaning or message. The most innovative ideas in the world will not make an impact if they cannot excite or move people.

In the context of the 4.0D® Leadership Development Model, we advocate two simple elements that should be contained in the story, the message or the lesson. The first element is Affect (emotion) and the second is Conation (behaviour). A point of departure to embark on the inspirational prowess journey is to formulate a personal aspirational vision in various forms:

- The first is to define oneself in the context of what kind of leader one aspires to be. Then, define the steps to achieve it.
- The second is to define one's personal legacy, envisaged in the form of what one would like significant other groups and individuals to say once one is not in this world anymore. These groups can be family, community members, colleagues, associates or members of a professional fraternity.

As people mature on their leadership journey, they must continue to tell stories with strong elements of behaviour ("what I have done or not done") and add emotional components to it ("lessons learnt, positive emotions, meaning derived").

Leaders who master the art of inspiring will have a great impact on people, and that will create followers; and leaders have followers, not employees. In the 4.0D® Leadership Development Model, inspiration serves as the foundation of the leadership element of having an impact on people, organisations and societies.

In our dealings with leaders, the majority indicate that, at some point in their lives, they had personal contact with someone who left an indelible mark of inspiration in their lives. It is very evident that even one single inspirational event can leave a lasting impression, so it is obviously very important for leaders to leave the right impressions to have positive impact on others or in organisations.

The A-C line: The interaction of the Affect with Cognition to grow Emotional Intelligence

"Outstanding leaders go out of their way to boost the self-esteem of their personnel. If people believe in themselves, it's amazing what they can accomplish."

Sam Walton

The resultant dynamic of the interaction between rationality and emotion is Emotional Intelligence (EQ). Leadership styles that would fit in with this dynamic line are the authentic and transactional leadership styles. A democratic bottom-up style of behaviour continuum would also fit in here.

While Chapter 2 dealt extensively with EQ, it never really had a "place" in leadership development in the sense that it was never comprehensively defined in the context of its contribution to leadership as a whole. The authors do also not agree with certain assertions that EQ equals leadership.

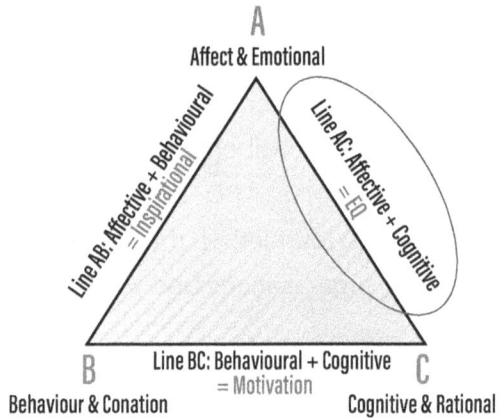

There is much more to it than merely one element with essentially the following four subcomponents:

- Identify own emotions (a cognitive diagnostic process in relation to emotion)
- Manage own emotions
- Identify the emotions of others (again a cognitive diagnostic process in relation to emotion)
- Manage the emotions of others

The above analysis implies that EQ is an element of leadership, and in the 4.0D® Leadership Development Model, it features well on the Cognitive-Affective (emotional) action line. In the context of the model, we have found a place for EQ in leadership in relation to many other elements and compass points. What is also evident is that EQ is an intra- and interpersonal aspect of human functioning. Therefore, it is only relevant in a people influence and interactive context. In this model, EQ serves as the basis for all leadership interactions between people.

The B-C line: The interaction of Behaviour with Cognition to effect Motivation

> *"Successful leaders see opportunities in every difficulty rather than the difficulty in every opportunity."*

Reed Markham

The outcome of conation & behaviour, combined with the outcome of the cognitive & rational infer leadership motivation (of the self, others, units or organisations). This is widely seen in the domain of the authoritarian and directive leadership styles.

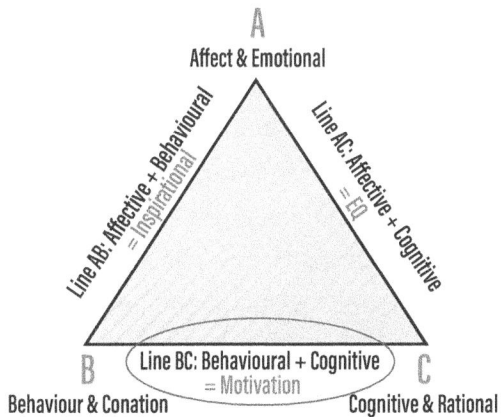

A

Affect & Emotional

Line AB: Affective + Behavioural = Inspirational

Line AC: Affective + Cognitive = EQ

B — Line BC: Behavioural + Cognitive = Motivation — C

Behaviour & Conation

Cognitive & Rational

Motivation is often confused with inspiration, but because the objectives of the two are different, it is useful for leaders to utilise it for other application opportunities. In its simplest form, inspiration leads to impact, where leaders aim to increase their number of followers. It is usually highly emotional.

Inspiration invariably describes a new horizon, condition or vista of some sort. Motivation, on the other hand, aims to get people to achieve a rational and understandable objective (that makes cognitive sense, such as a business case, goal or target). Motivation is a vital characteristic any leader should develop in order to serve the notion that leaders give direction, since motivated followers contribute towards achieving that direction.

In motivation, the leader alludes very strongly to the desired actions needed and energy inputs into the volition efforts (conation). This is evident during pep talks in sport, for instance, when the coach addresses the team at half time, telling them what they need to change, providing new tactics and ways to outfox the opposition to win the game.

To balance the three elements of the SELF (A, B and C), and at the same time keep the energy flowing between these lines (A-B, A-C and B-C) takes finesse. Only practice and consistent repetition will bring about a sound practice of these. A helpful tool to assess the dimensions of the model is the 4.0D® Leadership Assessment Protocol. A greater awareness of the elements of the SELF is a tremendous help for leaders in mastering the congruency and balanced interactions of the dynamics.

THE SECOND DIMENSION: THE THREE SIDE PANELS AND ASSOCIATED DYNAMIC LINES

Where Figure 14 showed the Action or Dynamic Lines in relation to the SELF, Figure 15 shows the base (shown in red and numbered as 1. The shape of the 4.0D® Leadership Development Model then postulates that three side panels arise from these dynamic lines into the tetrahedron shape.

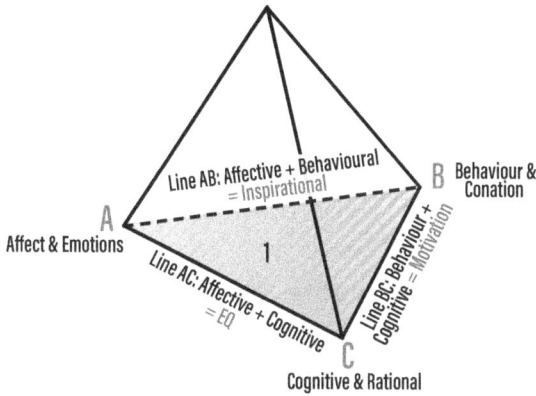

Figure 15: The position of the SELF in relation to the three panels

These panels are the WORK panel, the PEOPLE panel and the IMPACT panel.

In presenting these panels, we do so with a neutral disposition. Leaders who influence others by means of having impact (e.g. via inspiration), or who lead others to be successful (in a work context via motivation) and who have followers (e.g. via the Emotional Intelligence domain) will hopefully do so in a manner that is ethical, values based and morally acceptable in terms of the leadership Direction. It may happen that leaders have corrupted Directions, lacking morals and ethics, and thus the Impact, People influence and Work panels will bear negative and unacceptable consequence by normal standards. Thus, the 4.0D® Leadership Development Model also explains deviant leadership.

THE WORK PANEL

"The best leader is the one who has sense enough to pick good men to do what he wants done, and the self-restraint to keep from meddling with them while they do it."

Theodore Roosevelt

Action line B-C is the foundation of the WORK panel, in which Behaviour interacts with Cognition. This dimension, with motivation as the foundation, contributes to leadership that manifests in the context of the business environment, the internal environment of the organisation, the external environment, the business playing field and technical prowess. In Figure 16, the WORK panel is shown in purple and is numbered as Panel 2. It represents the vocational domain.

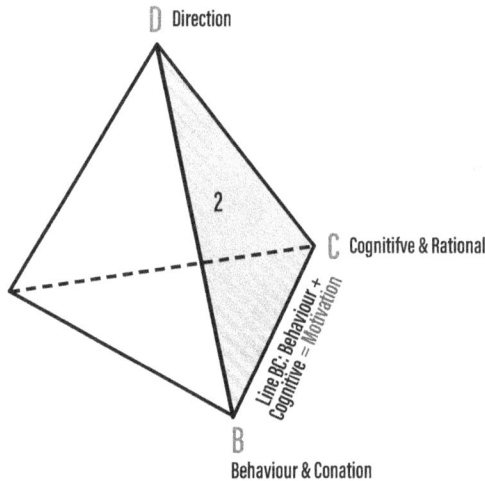

Figure 16: The WORK panel

THE PEOPLE PANEL

*"The greatest leader is not necessarily the
one who does the greatest things. He is the one that
gets the people to do the greatest things."*

Ronald Reagan

Action line A-C is the foundation of the PEOPLE panel and is the product of Affect interacting with Cognition. This social dimension encompasses leadership in the context of the interpersonal domain with reference to leading people and teams, formal and informal relationships, as well as building organisational culture. In Figure 17, the PEOPLE panel is shown in brown and is numbered as Panel 3.

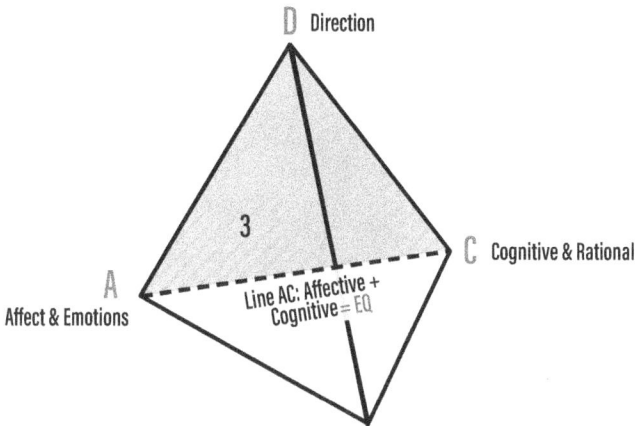

Figure 17: The PEOPLE panel

THE IMPACT PANEL

"If your actions inspire others to dream more, learn more, do more and become more, you are a leader."

John Quincy Adams

Action line A-B is the foundation of the IMPACT panel. It results from Affect interacting with Behaviour. This leadership dimension known as the IMPACT panel entails leadership in the context of inspiring meaningful impact on the community, internal and external stakeholders – whether they are antagonists or protagonists. It alludes to the leader's legacy on a variety of levels. In Figure 18, the IMPACT panel is shown in green and is numbered as Panel 4.

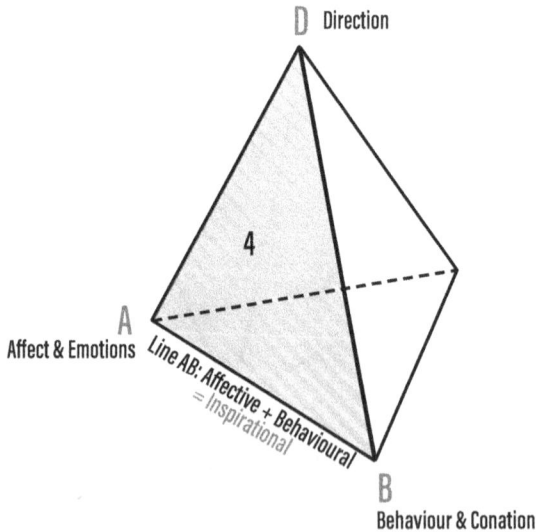

Figure 18: The IMPACT panel

THE THIRD DIMENSION: THE APEX

"A leader... is like a shepherd. He stays behind the flock, letting the most nimble go out ahead, whereupon the others follow, not realising that all along they are being directed from behind."

Nelson Mandela

The final dimension of the model is the Apex (labelled "D" in Figure 16), with the SELF as the base from which the three panels arise to join at the pinnacle of the tetrahedron, which represents leadership direction. The tetrahedron should ideally be comprised of congruent SELF, WORK, IMPACT and PEOPLE panels.

Congruency ensures balance, harmony and the seamless integration of the various leadership dimensions and elements of the panels. In the context of leadership direction, the Apex represents the unification of the SELF and the organisational direction in the form of the visionary futuristic dimension.

Each of the side panels has its own DIRECTION; therefore, the model accommodates the leader's directions in terms of the following:

- Direction towards which people should be guided via the organisational culture and values
- Direction of the organisational or business goals, vision, mission and objectives
- The directional objectives of the leader's impact on people, the organisation, societies, fraternities and possibly even beyond that.

- Direction encompasses leadership in the context of the future, with specific reference to the integration of personal and organisational visions, missions and values.

The volume within the pyramid also implies increasing levels of leadership complexity. To achieve optimal balance of the pyramid, leaders within organisations, executives and boards must formulate transparent, ethical, principled, virtuous and honest apexes or direction. This reflects value-driven leadership, supported by a sound base and three integrated panels. As mentioned previously, it can also happen that leaders may deviate from the norm of acceptable leadership, yet they are still leaders, albeit not acceptable in the legal, moral, ethical or values-driven criteria as desired by the reasonable man in society.

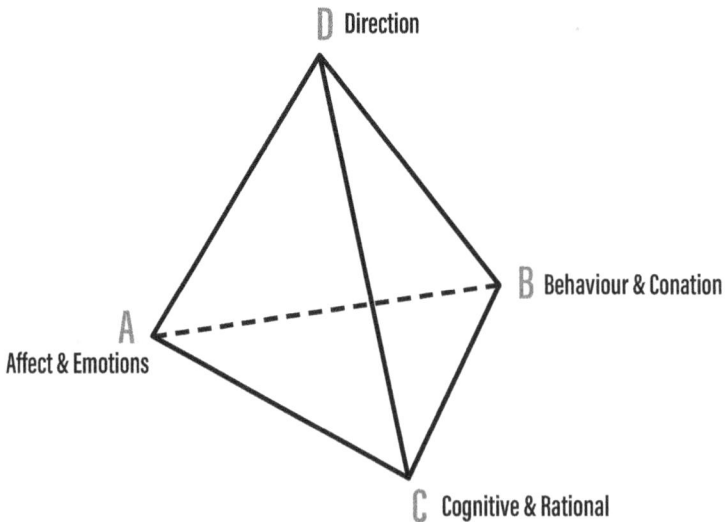

Figure 19: The 4.0D® Leadership Development Model

APPLICATION OF DIRECTION

*"The very essence of leadership is that you have to have vision.
You can't blow an uncertain trumpet."*

Father Theodore M. Hesburgh

Leaders develop vison to give direction to their people, their organisations or business, and themselves for their desired impact and legacy. The VUCA world makes it even more necessary today to provide followers with direction. In a VUCA world, where leaders pursue various leadership directions, they often face adversity, opposition, hardship, derailment and obstacles to achieve their goals and objectives.

This became very evident in working with leaders, and the first postulation of the model, in 2019, needed expansion to guide and enable leaders to discover their own potential and capabilities to overcome these negative influencing factors. In the latter part of 2019 and beginning of 2020, the model expanded and an article explaining its development and application was published in a peer-reviewed journal. The expansion entailed a description of the lines arising from the base to the Apex, termed the directional support lines. The directional support lines are critical in leadership survival, organisational endurance and business viability. These directional lines are critical support pillars for leaders' direction in challenging times.

A typical knock on effect of 4IR technologies is disruption. While disruption can go beyond technological origins and may stem from political events, environmental sources, biological and environmental causes, the central theme is survival. Herein lies the challenge for leaders and these directional support lines serve exactly that purpose.

While the model advocates a "bottom-up" approach, disruptions require a "top-down" intervention and action. When disruptions threaten personal or organisational directions, survival means that leaders must act with a sense of urgency. The top-down approach thus means to adjust the direction. By focusing on the three directional support lines, leaders can mitigate disruption. These directional support lines are Resilience, Agility and Flexibility/Adaptability.

THE A-D LINE: DIRECTION
- RESILIENCE AS THE AFFECT SUPPORT LINE

"Anyone can hold the helm when the sea is calm."

Publilius Syrus

The emotional (Affective) foundation of the A-D line translates into an individual or personal emotional capacity to recover quickly from difficulties and to attain a sufficient degree of emotional toughness.

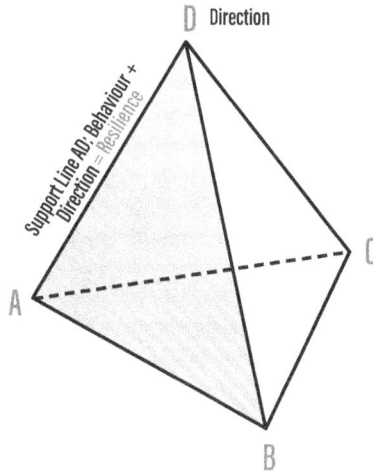

Figure 20: The A-D line: Direction – Resilience as the Affect support line

First described in 1973 and mistakenly classified as a trait, resilience is the result of an individual's ability to withstand stressful events to such an extent that they can restore their original psychological state after the event or episode. In view of every individual having different stress thresholds, adverse events will affect them differently. Highly resilient people also feel the intensity and impact of the event or problem. However, they have found effective ways to deal with it more quickly than others have.

Everyone can increase his or her resilience capabilities. Like any other human skill, learning greater resilience is something that everybody can do at any age. Resilience is not limited to any background, education or family relationship, and the only thing one needs is the motivation to do it. The American Psychological Association suggests 10 ways to build resilience.

These are the following:

1. Maintain good relationships with close family members, friends and others
2. Avoid seeing crises or stressful events as unbearable problems
3. Accept circumstances that cannot be changed
4. Develop realistic goals and move towards them
5. Take decisive actions in adverse situations
6. Look for opportunities of self-discovery after a struggle with loss
7. Develop self-confidence
8. Keep a long-term perspective and consider the stressful event in a broader context
9. Maintain a hopeful outlook, expecting good things and visualising what is wished
10. Take care of one's mind and body, exercise regularly, pay attention to one's own needs and feelings

Individuals can further reinforce levels of resilience through sound and healthy family relationships, establishing support systems such as problem-solving groups at work, maintaining a positive outlook in life and developing an attitude of transforming negative information in a positive way.

THE B-D LINE: DIRECTION – AGILITY AS THE BEHAVIOUR SUPPORT LINE

"The best way not to feel hopeless is to get up and do something. Don't wait for good things to happen to you. If you go out and make some good things happen, you will fill the world with hope, you will fill yourself with hope."

Barack Obama

The behaviour required to support direction during adversity entails leaders building personal capacity and dynamic capability to demonstrate behaviours that are reminiscent of "making a comeback" in VUCA environments and situations, and landing on one's feet when stumbling blocks or obstacles are encountered.

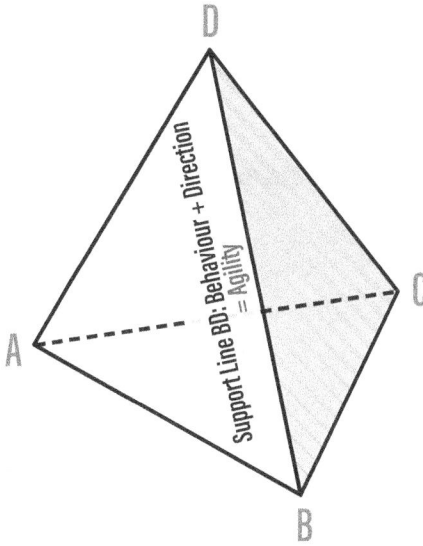

Figure 21: The B-D line: Direction – Agility as the Behaviour support line

Agile leaders have the ability to innovate and are able to jettison inappropriate skills and views. They replace their irrelevant ideas and change their perspectives. Part of the innovation is to challenge the current status quo of conventional thinking and assumptions. They offer best-practice solutions and original ideas and ways of doing things differently.

Apart from innovating, other skills most associated with agility are to take calculated risks, rise to the challenge and, once all is over, reflect introspectively on the lessons learnt.

Calculated risk-taking entails thinking things through well and pioneering to explore new opportunities and not thrill seeking. In challenging times, agile leaders will engage the issue and, during progress, learn new ways to behave and spontaneously modify previous behaviours. Once it is over, they naturally tend to reflect on the process and formulate alternative ways to address their blind spots and shortcomings.

The reason for their heightened reflective tendencies is that they are not defensive when challenged. In fact, agile leaders seem to use critical events and feedback to establish a newfound understanding of themselves, their problems and their situations.

THE C-D LINE: DIRECTION – FLEXIBILITY AND ADAPTABILITY AS THE COGNITIVE SUPPORT LINE

"Intelligence is the ability to adapt to changing circumstances; this is equally true for individuals, organisations, societies and nations."

Prof Reuven Feuerstein

The ability to listen and communicate appropriately, to negotiate well, to be open-minded and consider trends, and to adapt to changing circumstances demonstrates a sound flexible and adaptable capability. This assists leaders in pursuit of their directional goals.

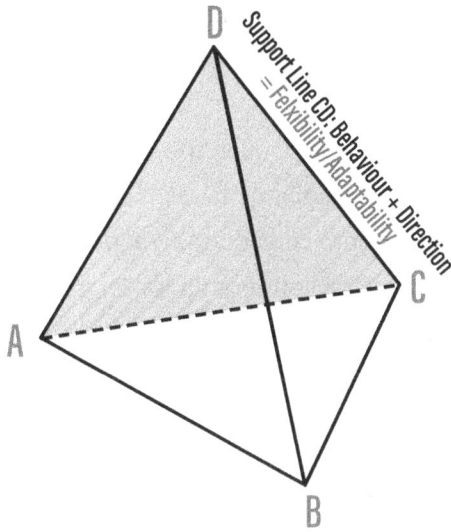

Figure 22: The A-D line: Direction
– Flexibility and Adaptability as the Cognitive support line

Cognitive flexibility is the mental ability to switch between thinking about two different concepts, and to think about multiple concepts concurrently. Cognition is one of the executive functions that differentiate humans from animals.

Two subcategories of cognitive flexibility are the following:

- **Task switching**: This is the mental process of *consciously* redirecting attention from one focus point to another.
- **Cognitive shifting:** This refers to the mental process of *unconsciously* redirecting attention from one focus point to another.

People with well-developed cognitive flexibility are able to solve complex problems and see relations between seemingly independent sets of information. The ability to apply cognitive faculties in a deductive and inductive reasoning sense also helps one to adapt and become flexible in pursuit of a goal.

Effective cognitive functioning implies the ability to process information accurately, storing and recalling it at required times. While the interpretation of information is a cognitive process, aspects such as personality, personal beliefs, leadership style, experience, aspirations, personal preference and many other factors will influence the nature and outcome of interpreting information.

Under the banner of cognition, the whole-brain approach means that the left hemisphere of the brain entails the logical, rational, tactile, judgmental, verbal thinking and factual aspects of cognition. The right hemisphere of the brain, on the other hand, holds the creative and intuitive elements, feelings, visualisation, imagination, colour and art.

Hemispherical dominance usually dictates in which mode a person mostly functions. Edward de Bono (1970) indicated that dominance of one hemisphere of the brain over the other is not a life sentence. By training the brain to achieve lateral thinking, both hemispheres apply equally. A few years before, in 1967, he proposed a five-day course in thinking. Of the many books De Bono published, it is evident that cognitive training and conditioning are possible, although it may take some effort.

PERTINENT POINTS FOR FUTURE APPLICATIONS OF THE 4.0D® LEADERSHIP DEVELOPMENT MODEL

"Life is like riding a bicycle. To keep your balance, you must keep moving."

Albert Einstein

The postulated 4.0D® Leadership Development Model is a model of balance of human dynamics of the SELF at the base and of the congruence of the arising panels. It integrates a variety of human elements into a working tool for the development of individual leadership elements that need reinforcement. It could also be used to identify individual leadership flaws and for diagnosing underdeveloped leadership dimensions.

If one or more panels are out of balance and/or the base is skew, sustainable leadership is adversely affected. An extreme imbalance can even cause the pyramid to topple over, and a disintegrating base will cause the "collapse" of leadership.

The leader and the organisation need to develop the ability to pay constant attention to the congruency between the panels. This will assist in monitoring leadership development as the complexity of the leadership role changes. The size ("volume" within the tetrahedron) of the 4.0D® Leadership Development Model should change accordingly.

The complexity of change results directly in changes to the required apex formulations that the leader must make. Thus, the apex of the CEO

133

requires a greater "volume" in the 4.0D® Leadership Development Model pyramid than the "volume" of the middle manager, whose apex will be tactical compared to the strategic apex of the CEO.

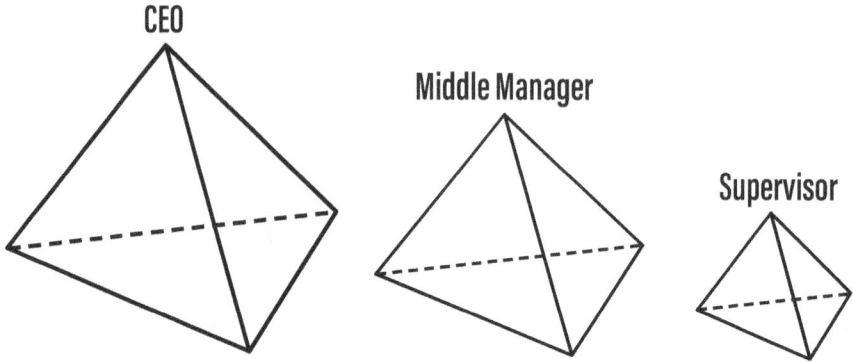

Figure 23: The 4.0D® Leadership Development Model in various complexity settings

The complexity of the inner space of the model is not only because the apex varies between operational and strategic contexts. To make this more understandable, we can consider Drotter's Leadership Pipeline, which illustrates this principle comprehensively. An individual's developments make all the lower and some of the higher passage postulations, depending on how far up in the organisation the individual can be utilised, promoted or advanced to:

- Passage 1: Managing self to managing others
- Passage 2: Managing others to managing managers
- Passage 3: Managing managers to managing a function
- Passage 4: Managing a function to managing a business
- Passage 5: Managing a business to managing a group
- Passage 6: Managing a group to managing an enterprise

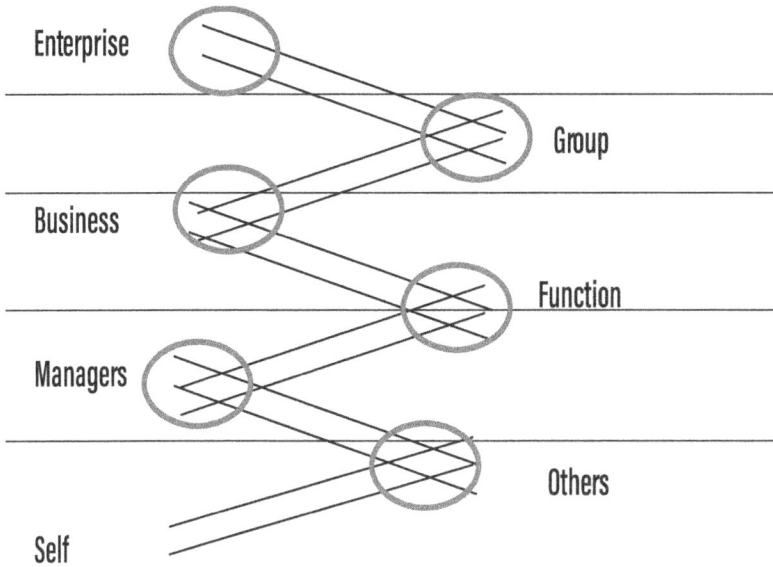

Figure 24: Drotter's Leadership Pipeline

In his leadership pipeline, Drotter asserts that, among other qualities and requirements, skills, time application and values will differ at each passage. The implication of these changes is also reflected in the 4.0D® Leadership Development Model in the following manner:

- **The SELF:** Many people may assert that the SELF, once formed and since it stems from Biology of the Three-Part Mind, must be static. We are at loggerheads with such a view because the dynamism of the human being from the biological to the psychological implies a fluid state and must therefore undergo growth, not only because of natural maturation, but also because of an accumulation of life experiences. All of these should lead to increasing wisdom and insights, and imply human affective, cognitive and conative growth and progression. Thus, the SELF, under normal circumstances, is destined to grow for as long as the human being is alive. The 4.0D® Leadership

Development Model, however, advocates a balanced growth and expansion. During leadership development journeys, this balance is constantly emphasised with the notion of congruence.

- **The Action Lines:** The three Action Lines – Inspiration, Motivation and EQ – should also increase in complexity if we consider them in the context of a leadership sphere of influence and width of impact. Whereas the appropriate EQ complexity practices between a leader and a small number of followers may be relatively easy to master and sustain, it becomes more complex if the context (and thus the diversity of people and cultures) changes; i.e. Leadership EQ in an organisation-wide (or global) context is vastly more complex than it is in a small group setting. The best arena in which this is repeatedly illustrated is politics and political leadership. Similarly, the same principle would apply for Motivation and Inspiration on a small (individuals or groups) to a large scale (organisation, national of global level).

- **The Directional Support Lines:** The three Directional Support lines – Agility, Resilience and Flexibility/Adaptability – are subject to the same scales as the Action lines. For instance, the Flexibility and Adaptability of a production plan for a department or function need a different leadership complexity than that required by the strategic imperative changes of an enterprise. The Adaptability and Flexibility challenges of an enterprise result from sudden yet complex Political, Technological, Social, Legal of Labour changes, and to change such an enterprise for survival and sustainability takes more complex Leadership steering. Again, the same principle will apply for the other two Action Lines as well.

The 4.0D® Leadership Development Model also aims to integrate a variety of separate points of leadership. While many programmes see EQ, for example, as the solution to leadership challenges, they rarely address the contextual fit with other human dynamics. The three dimensions and the elements of the 4.0D® Leadership Development Model offer an integrative approach. Since such an approach accommodates most of the leadership styles already discussed, it does not exclude any style, behaviour, contingency or trait.

In this regard, these may emanate from the "inner space" of the model. To assist in comprehending the inner space, the *4.0D® Leadership Development Model Visual Device* needs mentioning. The Visual Device is a physical tool that forms part of the model and is a tool to guide participants through the various elements of the model. It is initially in a "flat pack" state and, at some stage; attendees assemble the model into its tetrahedron form. The "inner space" then forms when the device transforms from a two-dimensional form to a three-dimensional one. We consider the inner space to be the crucible of leadership that may manifest in various styles, intrapersonal dynamics and psychological processes.

We believe that this inner space also provides room for developing or accommodating certain leadership types or approaches, such as Authentic Leadership (strongly linked to EQ) and Ethical Leadership (strongly linked to the morals and ethics of business conduct, as contained in values stemming from leadership direction), for example.

Click on the underlining to link and view an animated illustration of the 4.0D® Leadership Development Model Visual Device.

The mechanism of the inner space as a crucible for leadership is rooted in the SELF, and the dynamics of the SELF thus "rise up" into this inner space. As mentioned in Chapter 2, leadership is the business of people. We contend that the inner space of the model is the root of this people business or, as it is also known, co-constructive leadership. While there are three panels on the side of the development model, it is important to realise that the inner space is the fusion point that integrates all the panels of the 4.0D® Leadership Development Model.

Depending on the frame of reference from which one then considers leadership, the inner space is inclusive from a leadership developmental perspective. A number of leadership narratives are found in the recent body of knowledge, such as Empowered Leadership, Shared Leadership, Responsible or Ethical Leadership, and Servant Leadership, to name a few. As mentioned previously, the 4.0D® Leadership Development Model does not claim to cultivate any of the above. For instance, these will emerge as one of the potential leadership outcomes of the developmental model that are described in this book.

In any event, whatever may emanate from the inner space may subjectively seem to be private and only known to the individual. However, in Johari window[2] terms, there are also some things in blind spots, some hidden agendas and subconscious dynamics. In the context of the 4.0D® Leadership Development Model, however, it is very clear that, whatever is in the inner space, will visibly permeate to the "outside" of the SELF, IMPACT, PEOPLE and WORK panels of the model.

---

[2] *Johari window is a technique that helps people to better understanding their relationship with themselves and others. Psychologists Joseph Luft (1916-2014) and Harrington Ingham (1916-1995) in 1955 developed the concept and is used primarily in self-help groups and corporate settings as a heuristic exercise.*

We are hopeful that many debates will arise from the future applications of this model, such as the interplay between the leader as a person and the person as a leader (which is referred to in the next section). While we would welcome debates of this kind, we also advocate simplicity in a world of complexity. To this end, we simply assert, as we have done in the opening chapter, that real leadership development is about changing mindsets. This implies growing character, and developing, advocating and adjusting values. All these elements influence the SELF, which in the end, determines who we are as a person. To look at it in another way, true leaders are at ease with their leadership behaviours because of the SELF or congruence and subsequent actions that flow out of who they are as people.

Finally, the notion of being a leader or not being a leader is not really a choice anymore. As the full impact of the 4IR unfolds, it is envisaged that leadership will look different and that any form or level of decision, work practice and interaction between people will require some form of leadership, albeit on various levels and of varying span widths of influence in accordance with the complexity postulation discussed in this chapter.

THE 4.0D® LEADERSHIP ASSESSMENT PROTOCOL

"You need to assess yourself on a yearly basis and see how far you have gone and what you still need to work on."

Sunday Adelaja

The 4.0D® Leadership Assessment Protocol is an online process that generates a report of an individual's strengths and developmental areas on all elements and dimensions of the 4.0D® Leadership Development Model. Individuals assess their own ability on a Likert scale of 0 to 5 by specifying their level of agreement or disagreement on a symmetrical agree-disagree scale for a series of statements.

The report indicates, in detail, which specific areas are strengths that people can leverage in their individual leadership elements of the model. Conversely, the developmental areas also appear in the report, which is a developmental guideline for individuals to develop, improve or hone their leadership skills.

During the developmental process, the 4.0D® Leadership Assessment Protocol is the foundation of developmental focus. The results contained in the report not only speak to development, but are also offered graphically for each individual disposition in relation to the leader as person vs the person as a leader. The following figure is a graphic representation of the SELF in which the outer triangle represents the leader (maximum score that can be obtained) vs the person (actual measurement obtained). To close the gap is thus the objective that will feature in the developmental process and subsequent leadership journeys.

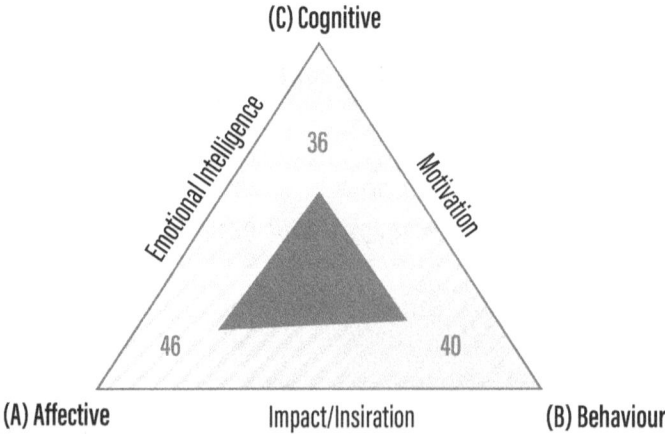

Figure 25: The SELF: Assessment results example

The 4.0D® Leadership Assessment Protocol, in combination with the 4.0D® Leadership Development Model Visual Device, is a useful tool in developing leaders for the 4IR. This book completes the toolbox as the third instrument towards future leadership.

CONCLUDING REMARKS

The 4.0D® Leadership Development Model is a new postulation, and through the peer-reviewed publications, we deem the epistemology as intact. The design stems from many decades of work in the leadership landscape, specifically in the mining industry, as well as manufacturing contexts.

Other pertinent points with regard to some important features of the model are the following:

- It is evident that, historically, there have been several different types and theories of leadership styles, each specific and relevant in terms of their time in history.
- In terms of the challenges associated with the 4IR and its expected complexities, a new type of Leadership Development Model needs to be postulated.
- The elements of the new 4.0D® Leadership Development Model include a base (SELF), which represents the intrapersonal dimensions of the leader, and three panels (the WORK, PEOPLE and IMPACT panels), which make up a triangular pyramid or tetrahedron.
- The basic components of any individual (or the SELF) lie within the psychological triad of Affect, Conation (Behaviour) and Cognition – the Three-Part Mind approach.
- A fundamental principle of the 4.0D® Leadership Development Model is that the interactive "balance" between Affect, Behaviour and Cognition (the A, B and C points of the congruent triangle) must

ideally be "perfect" (or at least strive to strike a synergistic balance between the aspects of the triad). Hence, the assertion is made that leadership starts with the SELF (the base of the model).

- The 4.0D® Leadership Development Model is the first Leadership Development Model that integrates several freestanding leadership compass points into a cohesive unit and places various important leadership requirements, such as EQ, Inspiration and Motivation, in context via action lines. These provide leaders with a clear "plan" or methodology to achieve these leadership requirements as the major elements define it very clearly.

- Through the directional support lines, the 4.0D® Leadership Development Model also clarifies the place of and need to develop new psychological "states of mind" for leaders and approaches to overcome adversity and obstacles in pursuing their personal and vocational visions and aspirations. In a VUCA world, through building resilience, practising agility and achieving better states of flexibility and adaptability, leaders should develop better coping strategies.

- The postulated 4.0D® Leadership Development Model is a model of the balance of human dynamics at the base and of the congruence of the rising panels. It integrates a variety of human elements into a working tool for identifying individual leadership flaws and for diagnosing underdeveloped leadership dimensions.

- The complexity of the changes taking place with increasing levels of leadership responsibility results directly in the required changes to the Apex formulations that the leader must make.

- It is the belief of the authors that the 4.0D® Leadership Development Model should be adopted at academic level as well to prepare future generations to deal with the complexities associated with the 4IR and beyond.

REFERENCES

Allport, G.W. (1937). Personality: *A psychological interpretation*. New York, NY: Holt, Rinehart and Winston.

Anderson, L.W. & Krathwohl, D.R. (eds.) (2001). *A taxonomy for learning, teaching, and assessing: A revision of Bloom's Taxonomy of educational objectives*. New York, NY: Longman.

Atman, K.S. (1987). The role of conation (striving) in the distance education enterprise. *American Journal of Distance Education*, 1(1), 14–24.

Bawamy, S. (2017). The future of leadership in the Fourth Industrial Revolution. https://www.hr.com/en/magazines/leadership_excellence_essentials/december_2017_leadership/the-future-of-leadership-in-the-4th%20-industrial-_jar4bzay.html.

Bagozzi, R. (1992). The self-regulation of attitudes, intentions, and behavior. *Social Psychology Quarterly*, 55(2), 178–204.

Bar-On, R. & Parker, J.D.A. (eds.) (2000). *The handbook of emotional intelligence: The theory and practice of development, evaluation, education, and application – at home, school, and in the workplace* (1st ed.). San Francisco, CA: Jossey-Bass.

Bar-On, R. (2006). The Bar-On model of emotional-social intelligence. *Psicothema*, 18, 13–25.

Bezuidenhout, A. & Schultz, C. (2013). Transformational leadership and employee engagement in the mining industry. *Journal of Contemporary Management*, 10(1), 279–297.

Blanchard, K. & Hodges, P. (2003). *The servant leader*. Nashville, TN: Thomas Nelson.

Blechman, E.A. (1990). *Moods, affect and emotions*. Hillsdale, NJ: Lawrence Erlbaum.

Bloom, B., Englehart, M., Furst, E., Hill, W. & Krathwohl, D. (1956). *Taxonomy of educational objectives: The classification of educational goals. Handbook I: Cognitive domain*. New York, NY: Longman.

Cabinet Office of Japan (2020) Society 5.0. Council for Science, Technology and Innovation. https://www8.cao.go.jp/cstp/english/society5_0/index.html.

Cag, D. (2020). 11 amazing examples of disruptive technology. https://richtopia.com/emerging-technologies/11-disruptive-technology-examples.

Chamber of Mines of South Africa (2017). *Modernisation: Towards the mine of tomorrow. Fact Sheet 2017*. Johannesburg: Chamber of Mines of South Africa.

Crimson Global Academy (2020) Top 10 jobs in 2030: Skills you should be developing! https://www.crimsoneducation.org/za/blog/campus-life-more/jobs-of-the-future/.

De Bono, E. (1967). *The 5-day course in thinking*. Middlesex: Penguin.

De Bono, E. (1970). *Lateral thinking*. Middlesex: Penguin.

De Bono, E. (1985). *Six thinking hats: An essential approach to business management.* Boston, MA: Little, Brown and Company.

Denton, M. & Vloeberghs, D. (2003). Leadership challenges for organisations in the new South Africa. *Leadership and Organization Development*, 24(2), 84–95.

Drotter, S. (2003). The leadership pipeline: The right leader in the right job. *The Management Forum Series*, 22 October 2003, Salem, ORE.

Edwards, L. (2010). Ronald Reagan and the fall of communism. The Heritage Foundation, USA. https://www.heritage.org/report/ronald-reagan-and-the-fall-communism.

Elkington, J. (2018). 25 years ago I coined the phrase "triple bottom line". Here's why it's time to rethink it. *Harvard Business Review*, 25 June 2018.

Gable, P.A. & Harmon-Jones, E. (2013). Does arousal per se account for the influence of appetitive stimuli on attentional scope and the late positive potential? *Psychophysiology*, 50(4), 344–350.

Gardiner, S. (2020). How the 5th Industrial Revolution is advancing humanity at workplace. https://www.fingent.com/blog/how-the-5th-industrial-revolution-is-advancing-humanity-at-workplace/.

Gauri, P. & Van Eerden, J. (2019). What is the 5th Industrial Revolution and why it matters. https://europeansting.com/2019/05/16/what-the-5th-industrial-revolution-is-and-why-it-matters/.

Goleman, D. (1995). *Emotional intelligence: Why it can matter more than IQ.* New York, NY: Bantam Books.

Goulston, M. (2009). *Just listen: Discover the secret to getting through to absolutely anyone.* New York, NY: AMACOM.

Gray, A. (2016). *The 10 skills you need to thrive in the Fourth Industrial Revolution.* Cologny: World Economic Forum.

Harmon-Jones, E., Gable, P.A. & Price, T.F. (2013). Does negative affect always narrow and positive affect always broaden the mind? Considering the influence of motivational intensity on cognitive scope. *Current Directions in Psychological Science*, 22(4), 301–307.

Hilgard, E.R. (1980). The trilogy of mind: Cognition, affection and conation. *Journal of Behavioural Sciences*, April, 107–117.

Howell, W.L. & Buckup, S. (2016). Leadership challenges of the 4th Industrial Revolution. https://www.weforum.org/agenda/2016/06/leadership-challenges-of-the-4th-industrial-revolution/.

Kolbe, K. (1990). *Conative connection.* Boston, MA: Addison Wesley Longman.

Kotter, J.P. (1990) *A force for change: How leadership differs from management.* New York, NY: The Free Press.

Lindsay, J. & Hudson, A. (2019) What is the fifth industrial revolution and how will it change the world? https://metro.co.uk/2019/06/10/fifth-industrial-revolution-will-change-world-9738825/?ito=cbshare.

Lonmin Platinum (2012). *Sustainable development report for the year ended 30 September 2012.* Retrieved from http://sd-report.lonmin.com/2012/people-planet-profit.

Maake, I. (2017). Take wat nie deur 'n masjien gedoen kan word nie [Tasks that cannot be done by a machine]. *Beeld*, 23 January 2017, 4.

Malnight, T. & Van der Graaf, K. (2011). Leadership challenges in South Africa: A land of contradictions. Leading in a connected future(LCF) insights #2011-004. https://pdfs.semanticscholar.org.

Marais, L. (2013). The impact of mine downscaling on the Free State goldfields. *Urban Forum*, 24, 503–521.

Maruping, P. (2012). *The mining sector innovation strategies implementation plan 2012/13–2016/17.* Pretoria: Technology Innovation Agency.

Matthews, G., Deary, I.J. & Whiteman, M.C. (2003). *Personality traits* (2nd ed). Cambridge: Cambridge University Press.

McClelland, D.C. (1961). The achieving society. New York, NY: Van Nostrand.

Motsoeneng, L., Schultz, C. & Bezuidenhout, A. (2013). *Skills needed by engineers in the platinum mining industry in South Africa.* Unisa. http://uir.unisa.ac.za/bitstream/handle/10500/13876/13R0045M%20Picmet%20Artikel_Motsoeneng.pdf?sequence=1.

Nicholls, J. (1994). The "heart, head and hands" of transforming leadership. *Leadership and Organization Development*, 15(6), 8–15.

Nichols A.L. & Cottrel, C.A. (2014). What do people desire in their leaders? The role of leadership level on trait desirability. *The Leadership Quarterly*, 25(4), 711–729.

PricewaterhouseCoopers (PwC) (2017). We need to talk about the future of mining. https://www.pwc.com/gx/en/energy-utilities.../pwc-mining-transformation-final.pdf.

Raza, A. (2019). 12 different types of leadership styles. https://wisetoast.com/12-different-types-of-leadership-styles.

Rosic, A. (2016). What is blockchain technology? A step-by-step guide for beginners. https://blockgeeks.com/guides/what-is-blockchain-technology/.

Salgues, B. (2018). *Society 5.0: Industry of the future, technologies, methods and tools.* Hoboken, NJ: Wiley.

South African Mining Extraction, Research Development and Innovation (SAMERDI) (2017). *Project charter: Human factors of the South African Mining Extraction, Research Development and Innovation (SAMERDI) strategy.* Johannesburg: SAMERDI.

Schultz, C. & Bezuidenhout, A. (2014). *A leadership initiative to enhance employee engagement amongst engineers at a gold mining plant in South Africa.* Unisa. http://uir.unisa.ac.za/bitstream/handle/10500/13883/Picmet%20artikel%20Leadership%20initiative%20_Anglo.pdf?sequence=1&isAllowed=y.

Scouller, J. (2011). *The three levels of leadership: How to develop your leadership presence, knowhow and skill.* Kemble: Management Books.

Sheppard, B.H. (2020). *Ten years to midnight: Four urgent global crises and their strategic solutions.* San Francisco, CA: Berrett-Koehler Publishers.

Sinek, S. (2009). *Start with why: How great leaders inspire everyone to take action.* The Strand: Penguin.

Smit, P., Cronje, G.J., Brevis, T. & Vrba, M. J. (2013). *Management principles: A contemporary edition for South Africa* (5th ed.). Cape Town: Juta.

Spillane, J.P., Halverson, R. & Diamond, J.B. (2004). Towards a theory of leadership practice. *Journal of Curriculum Studies,* 36(1), 3–34.

Stogdill, R. (1974). *Handbook of leadership: A survey of theory and research.* New York, NY: The Free Press.

Taylor, F.W. (1919). *The principles of scientific management.* New York, NY: Harper & Brothers.

Uys, J. & Webber-Youngman, R. (2019). A 4.0D Leadership Development Model postulation for the Fourth Industrial Revolution relating to the South African mining industry. *Journal of the South African Institute of Mining and Metallurgy.*

Uys, J. & Webber-Youngman, R. (2020). A 4.0D Leadership Development Model for mining and related industries in the context of the Fourth Industrial Revolution. *Mining Report Glückauf,* 156(1), 21–29.

INDEX

148

T

V

www.ingramcontent.com/pod-product-compliance
Lightning Source LLC
Chambersburg PA
CBHW071839200326

41519CB00016B/4170